RIDING The SKYLINE

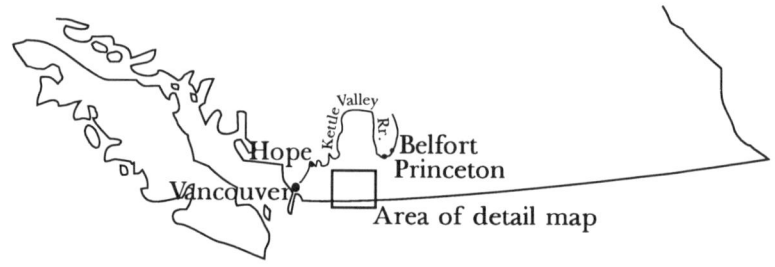

SOUTHERN BRITISH COLUMBIA

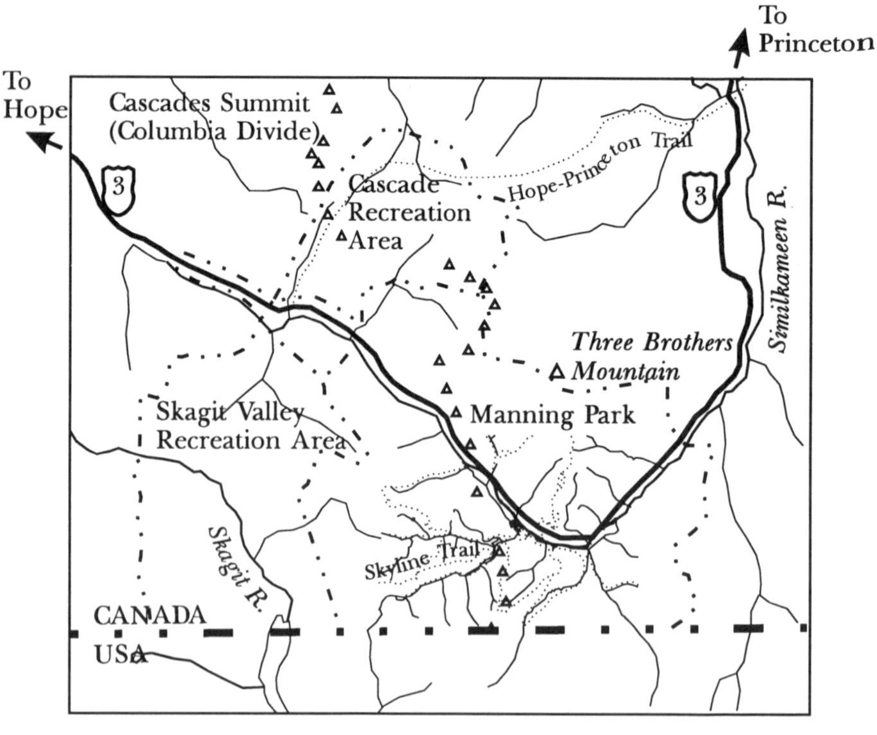

RIDING The SKYLINE

By M. Allerdale Grainger

Edited by Peter Murray

Horsdal & Schubart

Introduction copyright © 1994 by Peter Murray

No part of this book may be reproduced or transmitted in any form by any means, electronic or mechanical, including photocopying and recording, or by any information storage and retrieval system, without written permission from the publisher, except for brief passages quoted by a reviewer in a newspaper or magazine.

Horsdal & Schubart Publishers Ltd.
Victoria, BC., Canada

Cover photograph courtesy of Rupert Scheider, Toronto, hand-coloured by Bonnie Curran, Ganges, BC. Bert Thomas, left, Martin Grainger, centre, and Gus Murchy, right, on the Skyline Trail, 1919.

This book is set in Basset.

Printed and bound in Canada by Hignell Printing Limited, Winnipeg.

Canadian Cataloguing in Publication Data

Grainger, Martin Allerdale, 1874-1941.
   Riding the skyline

   ISBN 0-920663-26-5

1. Manning Provincial Park (B.C.) 2. Grainger, Martin Allerdale, 1874-1941. I. Murray, Peter, 1928- II. Title.
FC3815.M3G72 1994   917.11'5   C94-910162-1
F1089.M3G72 1994

CONTENTS

Introduction

Chapter One:	MY ESCAPE FROM BUSINESS	1
Chapter Two:	LETTERS, 1928	8
Chapter Three:	WITH HORSES IN THE WEST	25
Chapter Four:	LETTERS, 1929	34
Chapter Five:	DOWN SOUTH	54
Chapter Six:	LETTERS, 1930	56
Chapter Seven:	TRAVELLING LIGHT	68
Chapter Eight:	LETTERS, 1931	74
Chapter Nine:	THE SPIRIT OF THE WEST	98
Chapter Ten:	RIDING DOWN FROM CHILCOTIN	106
	Footnotes	114
	Index	118

INTRODUCTION

Martin Allerdale Grainger is best known as the author of *Woodsmen of the West*, a novel published in 1908 based on his experiences as a hand-logger on the British Columbia coast. Following its reissue in 1964 and 1983, *Woodsmen* has become recognized as a classic of early B.C. literature. Apart from occasional pieces of journalism which appeared in British newspapers and magazines, it is Grainger's only published writing.

But there was much more to Grainger's life in the province between his arrival as a young Cambridge University graduate during the gold rush of 1897, and his death in Vancouver in 1941. Some will recall that he played a leading role in the drafting of the first comprehensive forestry legislation in 1910.

Despite his lack of academic training — his degree was in mathematics — Grainger worked in the newly created Forest Branch and served as Chief Forester from 1916 to 1920 before following his predecessor, H.R. MacMillan, into the lumber business.

Less known is Grainger's ardent campaign to have the mountain country between Hope and Princeton preserved as a provincial park. He was among the first to recognize — as early as 1927 — that a proposed highway through the area would open up a spacious and beautiful playground for Vancouverites. He called it "Arcadia," after the mountainous area in Greece which came to denote a rustic paradise.

On May 20, 1928, the Vancouver *Daily Province* published a letter to the editor from Grainger which read in part:

> Various sports and amusements have been brought
> to British Columbia within the last fifty years, but the

Introduction

old-time Indians had one that takes a lot of beating — one suitable for man, woman or child. I mean camping and riding high up in the mountains in the Interior. Vancouverites who haven't tried this out are missing something.

You can take the train out of town any Friday evening, have two great days east of the mountains on trails, sleeping in camp, shack, ranch or hotel (whichever you prefer), and be back Sunday night. Bright sunlight and fine dry air up there are the right holiday change for anyone living on the Coast. You can ride horseback, drive around in cars, fish, picnic and wear old clothes, all in entirely different surroundings. With three days for your weekend trip instead of two, you can reach the great open region above 6,000 feet, with scenery equal to the world's best — real unspoiled old-time West. Take two or three days more (as in a summer vacation) and you can travel the alpine meadows at 7,000 to 8,000 feet.

The old-time Indians used to go into this high country early in the year and stay up there until the snow drove them out in the fall. 'Good place,' they said, *socalli illahi* — God's country. No business hustle up there.

In a brief notice enclosed with mailed copies of the letter, Grainger urged the formation of a "Skyline Club" to promote the area. He said a start had been made the previous year when a pamphlet had been circulated by his friend H.H. "Bert" Thomas of Princeton promoting "The Skyline Trail", a path along the southern boundary of the present Manning Park near the U.S. border. As a result, a number of well-known Vancouver citizens made trips in the region and became keen supporters of trail riding and mountain camping. Among the prominent people who explored the area on horseback and backed Grainger's campaign was MacMillan. Grainger concluded his notice by inviting those interested to send their names to his office so that "a committee could be formed and arrangements made for placing a fine B.C. sport on a proper footing (No subscription or money obligation of any kind is asked from anyone.)" There is no evidence that Grainger was overwhelmed by responses, however, and no record of a Skyline Club being formed. Nevertheless, he and Bert Thomas and others continued to lobby the government to have the area set aside.

The Hope-Princeton Highway wasn't completed until 1949 but in June of 1941, just four months before Grainger's death, the government finally acted to create Manning Park, named after another Chief Forester, Ernest C. Manning, who had been killed in an air crash earlier that year. Grainger's contribution was ignored at the time and he has never received the recognition he deserves. A booklet put out by the Ministry of Lands and Parks in 1991 marking the 50th anniversary of the park made no mention of Grainger's role. The only reminders in the park are Grainger Creek (formerly 33-Mile Creek) and the 21-kilometre Grainger Trail along the creek to Nicomen Lake.

The documentary record of his campaign of letters and petitions to preserve the area is contained in the provincial archives. Of more interest today is an evocative collection, also in the archives, of Grainger's writings expressing his joy in roaming the area on horseback. Mostly these took the form of letters to an old friend and business associate in England, C.F. Denny. A former senior partner in the firm of Denny, Mott and Dickson, which owned the Alberni-Pacific mill at Port Alberni managed by Grainger, Denny retired in his late 70s to his country estate near Croydon, south of London. Grainger's own business activities started to wind down in 1928 and went into a sharp decline when the Great Depression struck the following year. With time on his hands, he began to make more visits to his cabin on Bert Thomas' Princeton ranch, where his horses were stabled. Grainger began writing newsy letters to the old man, describing his expeditions on the trails and some of the interesting characters he met along the way. There were also digressions on winter trips made by Grainger and his wife to California, and the effects of the Depression in Vancouver and Princeton. Other articles recounted a horseback trip

Introduction

through the Chilcotin country and a local rodeo, as well as a train trip into the Rockies in Colorado.

Denny and his family were entranced by Grainger's vivid accounts and encouraged him to keep writing, with an eye to publication in magazines. Their enthusiastic response spurred Grainger on. "Years of restraint imposed in writing business letters and reports have made me suffer from suppressed writer's itch," he told Denny in an early letter.

Grainger's father had started out as a newspaperman and the son's first byline appeared during the Boer War when, as a 26-year-old soldier, he wrote a number of "news-letters" from the front to the *Daily News* of London. He used the name "M. Allerdale Grainger" on these dispatches and later for *Woodsmen of the West* and other writings on forestry matters. In keeping with this practice it has been adopted for the present book. Allerdale ("Allie") was his father's name but the son was known as Martin — "Mart" to his friends, and "Monnie" to his family.

Grainger followed his Boer War dispatches with a few newspaper and magazine articles, but after the publication of *Woodsmen* he wrote little except on forestry matters. There were also many private and business letters, and a colleague said that a letter from Grainger "was a thing to be prized." This admirer called Grainger a "natural writer", but another business associate described him as a perfectionist who painstakingly rewrote and polished his correspondence.

This dedication to craft is evident in Grainger's letters to Denny and his niece Evelyn Grey, as well as in the sketches written between 1928 and 1931 included here. They were given to the archives by Evelyn and consist of copies of originals typed by Grainger's secretary, Dorothy Browning, who became virtually a business partner and looked after the office during his frequent absences. Some of the letters carry dates and bear the name of the recipient, while others have no salutation. A few which Grainger titled were obviously not intended as letters. One, headed "My Escape From Business", was apparently meant as an introduction for publication of the collection.

Grainger wrote swiftly. He composed many of these letters and essays on the Kettle Valley train back to Vancouver from

Princeton, wrote them out in longhand, then turned them over to Miss Browning for typing. There is no evidence of extensive rewriting, although there are two versions of some articles. Some rough spots remained and I have taken the liberty of acting as copy editor, making a few cuts and changes, mostly in punctuation. Grainger wrote during this time as if he had just discovered the semi-colon, piling them up in sentences that seemed to go on forever. These have been altered, in some cases with the substitution of commas, in others with the insertion of periods.

Apart from these minor changes the collection represents the quintessential Grainger: witty, wise, self-deprecating, iconoclastic — his decency and integrity always evident. (Only in his attitude toward Central European immigrants did Grainger betray some of the common racial bigotry of the time, and to Denny he expressed, not surprisingly, a pro-British, anti-American bias.) But Grainger was a fan of the American radio philosopher and humourist Will Rogers, admiring his "delightful caustic comments." Closer to home, Grainger will remind readers of Paul St. Pierre. Grainger put his stamp on the countryside and people of Princeton just as St. Pierre has done for the Cariboo. (Both men, it should be noted, abandoned for a time their deep-rooted independence by entering the confining worlds of, respectively, business and politics.)

As his friend Norman Spalding observed, Grainger "was the kind of man you did not have to get to know, you admired and respected and loved him at once." We can only know him through his writings, and I hope this addition to his published work will lead more people to appreciate Martin Grainger as an engaging writer, a fine man and an outstanding British Columbian.

Peter Murray
Victoria, 1994

Chapter One

MY ESCAPE FROM BUSINESS

"What for, all-the-time white man work?"
Eagle Lake Jimmy

I have always disliked Business. I came West, in 1897, on the Klondike Rush, to avoid it. And here, a quarter of a century later, I was in a city office, buzzing my life away like a fly in a trap. I lived among people with whom it was the unquestioned thing that a man should be at his place of business early and late, day in day out, his mind occupied with the process of making money — one job, problem or discussion after another, endlessly.

He should invite people to the Club for lunch and talk business between mouthfuls; he should let his body soften in trade meetings, office conferences, hotels, trains, car journeys, and spend countless hours talking shop with other men or battling with papers on a desk and entries in a notebook, slumped in a chair with his insides sagged down, his eyes overtired, his nerves in high tension from urgencies, emergencies, hurry, indigestion, interruptions, telephones, telegrams, callers, factory clatter, street noises, typewriters. Should work demand it, he must go back to his office in the evening and at weekends, give family life the go-by, ignore his friends and cancel summer holidays without a qualm. "This is a crucial year," he must say, and let Business override all else.

While I myself earned a living in this way, there were lucid moments in which I would ask my city friends why they lived the lives they did. Some would answer that they got great pleasure from it. These were men of astute judgment, smart traders or skilful executives. They liked to exercise their special abilities and thus to make money. For them each day was full of entertainment.

"Tell me," said one, "what is there in life that can compare with the interest that a man takes in his own business?" It was in this spirit, "because he liked to see his money working," that old Tom Whatcom, at 77, plowed back a million dollars cash into a new timber venture and lost the lot. He could not be happy without the daily troubles of a logging camp, bad markets and loans from exasperated banks. But the shrewder among my friends thrived on this diet and made money.

With other men, vanity was plainly the driving power — the ambition to be prominent citizens, with the prestige and vague feel of power that success in money-making gives. "Why don't you quit business?" I asked Bill Haynes. "You've got enough."

"What is enough?" he asked. His wife broke in. "I'll tell you," she said, for she was tired by too much business-hospitality. "Enough is the carrots that are tied to the stick that is tied to the donkey's head." But Bill was convinced that there could be no half way — either you went full blast, outdoing your competitors, or else they submerged you.

Nearly all the men I knew thought that they lived the industrious termite life because they had to; there were wives and children to be provided for; there was fear of the future; moreover, what else was there to do since a man must spend his life in work anyway, or go to pieces? Body and soul could not be maintained on golf. How my venerable father would have disliked this point of view, he who started me out in life with the impressive maxim, "Always remember, Martin, there was never any money made yet by hard work." Speculation, in West Australian mining stocks, was what he himself believed in.[1]

Well, I was certainly making little money by neglecting my father's advice. Though Business and the dentist looked alike to me, I drove myself to work with desperate intensity, to the very limit of endurance, in much bodily discomfort and bored stiff. I even took to philosophy (that last refuge in defeat), reading Marcus Aurelius and sending little extracts from him,

My Escape from Business

neatly typed, to vary the office correspondence read by my associates. To lessen the pain of meeting new-made millionaires at the Club, I would cut verses like this from newspapers:

"...some of them make it
and some of them lose it,
but all of them die
before learning to use it."

And when ailments took me on a round of the best-known clinics, I preserved this saying of a nerve specialist: "We are the boys who see the underside of the high voltage American Business Life. They come to us in droves, with arthritis, rheumatism, phobias, melancholia, indigestion, eyestrain, and other, less dressy results." It was all very depressing, just as in Purcell's time, three hundred years ago:

"Why so serious, why so grave
Man of business why so muddy?
Thyself from ill thou cannot save
With all thy care and study ..."

So I ruminated, one bright day in June, knowing (like R.L. Stevenson) that I could never afford to earn much money — it would cost me too much. The office was hot and stuffy. The clacking of typewriters rose to a whirr whenever Miss Browning joined in with hers; telephones buzzed, traffic noises came through the windows.[2] There was Trouble in the mail and Trouble by wire from our sawmill manager. Several visitors had got through the entanglements of the outer office and wasted my time. Ever since 8:30, I had been trying to write overdue reports to catch the mail for England. Now they were done, I had eyestrain and a bilious headache. All the delights of high-speed business were mine.

Outside, above the heated buildings, I could see through the office window a snow-white cloud or two floating in the blue sky. The mountains across the harbour looked magnificent — usually I would never notice them. Seagulls flashed above the moving ships. It seemed to me a shame to be shut away from a man's natural life out there in the open, fussing with one's brains in a feverish office. The human body is a republic of many billion cells formed during eons of time by physical exertion under the open sky. If you cut out the physical exertion and over-excite a few brain cells your republic is in danger of revolt. So I was reflecting when Miss Browning brought in a basketful of incoming mail. I picked up the top letter and this is what I read:

Vermilion Forks[3]
June 6th, 19—

Dear Grainger:
I came here yesterday and am staying with Ranger Norton, inspecting some cuttings of Government timber by the railway. There is fine mountain country around here that you can get near to by train in eight hours from the Coast through the Coquihalla Pass. Norton says that horses are plentiful and can be bought for $60 up. The larger they are the more you have to pay. For $100 you can get a good sound animal. Some of them are kind of wild and snorty but Norton says he could pick up some that would be what he calls plum gentle and the sort a man wants for going camping with. Norton says the trails over the mountains are not open yet owing to snow on the summit, but by July 1 a person could get across. A pack outfit is necessary as there is no one living in that country. You ought to come and see these parts. There are very few mosquitoes round here and the weather is real hot.

Yours sincerely, W. Hemingson.

*

Well, here we were, the horse and I, jogging along the old Hope trail. It had been blazing hot down below when we made our belated start from the little mining town and rose some miles through park-like rolling country, but now at higher

My Escape from Business

elevation a jackpine forest shaded us. The trail was dusty and made soft footing for the horse. There were recent hoof-prints which I had been told to follow should they leave the trail, for Ranger Norton and two friends were in the mountains somewhere up ahead and would wait for me to join them.

Before coming on the trip, I had spent an hour or two in the provincial archives, reading about early days in this mountain country. One booklet published in San Francisco in 1857 gave two routes for gold-seekers of that time who should wish to venture far north, into what was then the wilderness of British Columbia. The best way, said the booklet, was to take the boat from San Francisco to the Columbia River, then go upstream to the head of navigation. At this point the gold-seeker must get pack-horses. In 27 days, 380 miles, he would, with luck, reach Fort Kamloops, a trading post of the Hudson's Bay Company, and enter gold-bearing country. Or, said the booklet, he could sail up the Pacific Coast to the Fraser River, go up it a hundred miles to the mouth of a wild canyon and there await the chance that one of the occasional trains of pack-horses might come across the mountains and carry his stuff into the Interior on the return trip. Pick and shovel, axe and gold pan he would have, as well as bedding, clothing and some sort of tent, flour, sugar, beans, salt-pork or bacon, maybe a rifle. Plenty of food was urged upon him because game was over-hunted by the Indians and man could not live upon the country.

In the archives, too, I saw the early maps on which mountain ranges and rivers were drawn in queer directions and there were great blanks where now are settlements and highways. But you could see that trappers and miners and the fur-trade men had been to many places even 90 years ago. When Great Britain ceded territory to the United States, the Hudson's Bay Company had been forced to find new outlets to the sea; trails were made across the Cascade Mountains down to the head of navigation on the Fraser River. During two years, in the late forties, pack-horses even forded the Fraser at low water, an astounding thought to anyone who knows the wicked look of that great river below Hell's Gate. But this feat proved too dangerous even for the tough old-timers, and they made safer trails to a little place called Hope.

And so by 1860 the trail on which I was riding came into being, sixty-six miles long between settlements and rising to 6,000 feet. Miners used it in the excitements of the sixties, seventies, eighties. Herds of cattle were driven over it. Only when the C.P.R. was built in 1887 did it cease to be the chief thoroughfare from British Columbia's coast to the Southern Interior; by the turn of the century travel over it had fallen to a trickle. Nowadays, after the summit snow melted in June, a few prospectors would use the trail, a few cowboys take horses to market on the Coast, there would be a camper or so, like myself, a few fishermen and hunters. Then cold Autumn would come, Winter would pile snow high and the trail be left untravelled, except here and there by a lone trapper, foxes, coyotes, cougars.

This Cascade country is full of deep gulches between hills. The horse and I would travel for a mile or two along a high flat bench, zig-zag down for half a mile to cross a creek, climb again, cross another flat, go down and up again, hour after

Along the Hope-Princeton trail, Martin Grainger at left, Bert Thomas centre, 1919. (COURTESY BC ARCHIVES AND RECORDS SERVICE)

My Escape from Business

hour. The horse, wiry and surefooted, used to such country from its birth, stood the work well. I, soft city man, did not. My skin chafed against the saddlery, my joints ached from unaccustomed exercise; soon I was dismounting and leading the horse whenever the trail dipped downhill. There were flounderings in little bogs, too, that delayed us and the crossing (or getting round) of old log bridges rotted by the years; the saddle blankets kept shifting and the hungry horse snatching at tufts of grass. Dusk came on before we had reached the summit. I saw the mouldering remains of an old corral fence beside a creek, evidently a stopping place for pack trains in days gone by, and there made camp. This was simple, for the air was warm. I tied the horse to a tree after a feed of oats; unrolled my little quilt on a mattress of dry pine needles, put the saddle for a pillow and turned in, boots and all, under the brilliant stars, too tired to light a fire or eat.

The horse slept noiselessly. Dim shapes of trees, bolt upright, pointed to the sky, motionless, regiment upon regiment of them. There was dead silence in all the world. It was uncanny. Lying awake idly watching the sparkling universe above, I was amused to feel what very little things business worries in a far-off city really were, a well-worn sentiment otherwise expressed by the astronomer who began a magazine article like this:

> From the viewpoint of astrophysical studies of the Universe, Life is not an important matter. It is but one among many phenomena upon the surface of a planet which itself is but a fragment of secondary importance. Civilizations and other animal manifestations are but parasites upon photo-synthesis — that process in the leaves of plants in virtue of which we are all breathing, living and thinking.

I used to keep that quotation on my office desk to edify business visitors.

Chapter Two
LETTERS, 1928

March 30, 1928
Dear Mr. Denny:

 I greatly appreciate your letter. If my little chronicles of local life interest you I am delighted to repeat them. Years of restraint imposed in writing business letters and reports have made me suffer from suppressed writer's itch so that, when you incautiously give encouragement, you may let loose too much scribbling and be bored. However, I will risk that in view of your kind remarks.
 About Friday last week the wear and tear of business began to get me, so in the afternoon I wired to Princeton to ask about the weather. The answer was "Plenty snow and mud round Princeton but side hills are partly clear for riding." I went home, put on some rough clothes and just caught the evening train.[4]
 About four in the morning, just as the sky was lightening in the East, the train dropped me and my pocket lantern on a high hillside. I walked about half a mile and looked down upon the little flat which is Bert Thomas' ranch.[5] A few horses and cattle were straying around but no one was up, so I went down and across the snow-covered fields to a comfortable-looking haystack where I joined company with three rabbits, half a dozen awakening fowls, a cow with a just-born calf, and two sleepy saddle horses that I knew. The air was fairly sharp at that elevation of 2,200 feet at this early season of the year, so I dug a hollow in the haystack and finished my night's sleep there. Then I lit a fire in a little copse and warmed myself until signs of life in the ranch house took me over to the

Letters, 1928

kitchen, where I became one of a miscellaneous mob of fourteen, mostly children.

George Allison was there, wild-haired (I've never seen him with a hat), weather-tanned, rough-clothed, as full as usual of enthusiastic life. Even at breakfast conversation started on the mining boom, for George has spent his life in the high mountains prospecting for gold, silver, lead, coal, and what not. He is a bachelor, has a small mob of horses who are great friends of his, and is one of the finest outdoor men I have ever seen. Both he and his sister's husband (my friend Bert Thomas) love the mountain country *and* horses. Horses and prospecting keep them poor — sad result of motor cars and gasoline, for in the old days theirs was a great horse country and I have a vivid memory of Mrs. Thomas, with hair flying, cleaning up events at cowboy race meets on "Jimmy", the old ex-racehorse from California whom they bought for a song with a damaged knee (which they cured by nursing) and smuggled through the mountains. There are usually a mob of horses lounging round the house and stables, or drinking at the pretty little stream that runs through the yard. Milk cans stand in the water knee deep to keep cool, among the ducks and fish. A little way up the stream there is a beaver dam which some brute broke last year, and George used to spend quite a little time in cutting saplings and helping the old beaver to rebuild. He told me they got on quite friendly terms with each other.

George's mind was bursting with thoughts of coal. "Do you remember, Grainger, when you and Mr. Macaulay and your friends camped one night at Nine-Mile Creek?[6] Bert and I had uncovered a ledge of coal about 400 yards from the camp and I wanted to take you people up and show it but Bert said 'Don't do it, they might think we wanted to sell them a wildcat,' so we didn't. It was costing us $125 a year and we hung on for several years unable to interest anybody so we let it go for $500. The feller we sold it to got $50,000 the other day. They have drove in a tunnel 500 feet, have got an eleven-foot seam and are shipping eight tons a day to Vancouver. One of the coal men from Fernie has just paid $50,000 for coal rights on two square miles towards Princeton. Within a mile of this range a small outfit from Spokane have got a nine-foot seam as I know, for I looked into their tunnel one time when they were away. That seam is heading straight for the hills where you got off the train just now and here's the geological map showing sandstone formations all through them. The horses are ready, come on up and see."

So we wrapped in heavy coats for the wind was chill. I could hardly recognize the horses in their thick winter coats but they were in good condition, as their horses always are, and we had a great ride over the hills, George stopping every once in a while to use his prospector's pick on limestone outcrops. We made a bonfire out of an old fallen tree and warmed up, as the wind was cold, then back for supper and more maps. Bert and George have been hanging on for many years to a bunch of copper claims that are within a stone's throw of the Granby mine on Copper Mountain which ships 2,500 tons of rock a day to its concentrator. The company has plenty of ore in sight and will be in business for a century, and it can have these claims at its own price any time from people like Bert and George who find it hard to pay their yearly taxes and are getting older all the time. But George, as Bert explained, is now "on velvet," for after many years of empty pockets, someone actually paid him $2,500 the other day for a claim on Kennedy Mountain. His spirit is always fine. Of the lost coal mine he said, "I never give it a worry, I need all my thinking to go after the next one."

What horsemen these fellows are. George and a friend, on saddle horses, with pack-horses, went into the high mountains last month to stake some wildcat claims on the ground around somebody else's previous staking, just in case there might be something there. (George has the claims bonded to somebody now for $90,000, but he does not really expect to get anything at all.) They travelled on top of packed snow eight feet deep. In such places there would be soft holes where the tops of little trees came near the surface and at first the horses kept falling into these, with much floundering to get out. They got wise pretty soon, George said, and thereafter seemed to smell the soft places and avoid them. George said the queer shapes of the high peaks, all muffled up in snow, were a great sight. He has an artist's appreciation of these matters, which reminded him about anthracite because he and Bert had found a ledge of what they thought was anthracite away over on the headwaters of the Little Muddy, and there were a couple of big salt licks back of Skaist Mountain which they thought must be potash and did I know what potash looked like? If only some of these fellers in Vancouver would put up a little money for a fellow to do a little development work on a little silver-lead proposition they had near the Coquihalla Pass, George believed that it might be worth their while, although of course he could not guarantee results.

George has made many trips as guide for the Canadian Geological Survey. He can talk rock formations with the best of them. We went on late into the night planning mountain trips for coming Summer — pipe-dreams most of them.

Next day they ran me into town, along hill roads with muddy ruts two feet deep, with the little Ford engine roaring its head off. So I caught the evening train and, avoiding the smug pullman, passed several pleasant hours in the day coach forward where the guard, two old men and myself passed around samples of rock and talked mining (they took me for some sort of mining person), and Chinese railway labourers gabbled on their way to town and holiday, the life of the country carrying on around one as men with packs and blankets, ranchers and women with their families got on and off at little wayside stations in the hills. When they stopped to change engines at Hope, I walked back of the train and had the last glimpse of the towering mountains we had come through, and the blazing stars and new moon that we so seldom see in this misty coast atmosphere. Two days in the peaceful tranquil mountains, a complete release from the unceasing fussiness of city life.

* * *

May 22, 1928
Dear Evie:[7]

When I was crippled in 1914 the bottom fell out of my world. Month after month, those feet of mine were just wrecks.[8] 1914 became '15, then came '16, '17 — you remember how it was. Many a time, to a person devoted to physical activity and then already in his forties, it seemed like The Finish. Looking back now it is of course quite clear that such lugubrious ideas were a mistake. In any smash-up of that kind there are usually the makings of a new world — a bit smaller than the old one maybe but fine and dandy all the same. When you see MacMillan careering over mountain sides to photograph wild goat, or Andrews doing three men's work in charge of the largest logging camp in B.C., you can see that lying up with T.B. for some months (tedious, wearisome, boresome as it inevitably is) does not shut off a vigorous future from those people who really go after it.[9] Even lying up can become a sort of indoor sport after a person gets the big idea and the technique of how to do it. After ten months of it once, as a small boy, I remember being quite sorry to leave a hospital, rather like the leper attendant I may have told you about, who, when our steamer was passing Leper Island (that unholy, bare, windswept sandspit with its gaunt buildings, at the entrance of Cape Town Bay) turned to me and said, "Well, there's the dear old place" and giggled happily.

You will be back on the Skyline, like MacMillan, in a year or so. Maybe you will have to live a lot on horseback, among mountains, so meanwhile I will keep you posted as to what is going on up there. Remember this too, that people like you and Dart and myself, and other good friends we know, who have stuck to regular exercise for years, have a tremendous pull in battling against illness.[10] Their 500 billion cells have innate healthiness.

On the new big motor ferry *Princess Elaine* I breakfasted Friday morning with Pendleton Senior, Ross, and Jack MacMillan.[11] I had been over to Alberni the day before with

VanDusen and his manager from Japan to discuss Jap squares and other delicatessen of the lumber business, such as the quantity of lumber per gang hour that Alberni stevedores stow into vessels (which averages 10.8, VanDusen says, instead of something else that he would like).[12]

After breakfast we ruined two hours of bright sunshine, blue sea and airy, green islands and white distant mountains, by inhaling each other's cigars in earnest discussion as to whether or no Alberni should join the new selling company the sawmills are forming. Nine-thirty saw us erupt into the office, shattering Miss Browning's day thereafter with incessant jangling phone and buzzer calls; four phones going full blast; callers to be seen and callers butchered by trusted Dragons guarding us; all the fussomalorums you grin at when you visit our little fairy grotto, 713 Metropolitan Building.[13] John Lafon was leaving that evening on a long business trip to the Interior; there were alarums between H.R. MacMillan and the sawmill folk about the selling company with which I somehow became mixed up; there was this and there was that — every kind of rush — till at 6:40 I bolted for home in a taxi and your father watched me grab a meal while we telephoned Dr. Strong and drafted a cable to your Honolulu doctor in reply to one about you that had come mixed with our business cables earlier in the day.[14] At 7:05 your Aunt phoned for a taxi; we piled in bundles of camp stuff; porters at the station ran with these bundles; the starting gong rang; we settled breathlessly in our seats on the Kettle Valley train just as 7:30 struck.

*

The stars were bright as I turned over in the new, double-pocket feather quilt, certainly the warmest thing I have ever slept in. A few minutes later as it were, dawn filled the sky, then mist hung motionless on the alfalfa fields, budding leaves on trees above my bed were still. Profound peace — just a tiny murmur on the creek and cawing of distant crows waiting to grab young turkey chicks over at Alf's place further down the flat. Four a.m. and breakfast time. How delightfully easy to roll out already dressed, shove on soft moccasins, take a handful of dead leaves and twigs to start a campfire, hang a billy to boil and prop up bread to toast. Ten calendar minutes to hot coffee and delicate cold-boiled rice taken plain, warming oneself crouched on the ground before the blaze, like a tramp. A good new-born day with hectic yesterday and its worries blotted out and horses across the creek whinnying.

Then Dixie. Bert tells me that the first time they ever saddled her was on a wild morning years ago when they had sheep on the high summits late in the Autumn. It started snowing heavily and for a desperate hour or two there was doubt whether the sheep could be driven down before the snow would bog them. The horses were loaded anyhow, in a hurry, shooed down the trail for home and then forgotten. Hours after, when the sheep had been saved, Bert caught up to Dixie waddling contentedly along the trail with saddle and clumsy pack underneath her tummy. Think of the fireworks you and I have seen when saddles slipped that way!

The first furniture in our shack was a sack of oats, and this made a great hit with the horses, who probably have not eaten oats a dozen times in their lives. The sight of me half a mile away stirs their thoughts at once. There is a little corral among the big trees just behind our shack and the boys leave the horses there whenever Dart and I are expected from Vancouver. The shack is fine: 24' x 12' inside, with a side veranda 10' x 12' where saddles hang on walls with pack bags, hobbles, cinch ropes and every sort of camp stuff. Chipmunks flip in and out and steal our oats; bluebirds are nesting a few feet away. Dart sleeps in the cretonned-alcove portion of the shack; the rest is living-room, with a five-dollar, sheet-iron cooking stove in tender memory of Klondike days. The stove, all the same, will knock spots off any heavy metal affair there is — for speed of cooking. It goes red hot in a whiff of time. No tiresome delay while you eat bread and wonder what on earth the waiter can be doing. Hot food, on the spot, the way you want it, when you want it. A woman likes an indoor stove; for me the tramp's fire outside with posts suspended by wire hooks from a cross stick between two uprights.

Herbert Heald "Bert" Thomas. (COURTESY BC ARCHIVES AND RECORDS SERVICE)

They brought me Sam (the stocky little horse that toasts itself so at campfires) when I was up there one weekend, because Dixie and the others had broken through a fence and gone up-range. Sam is one of the few horses belonging to George that a person like me dares to get upon. The others, as Bert puts it, are all right as long as you let them do what they want.

Well, well, small boy Bill on Skidoo very portly with Spring grass fat, and myself on Sam, went up Five-Mile Range. All nature was smiling and gay, the high swelling hills a symphony in green major, with blazing masses of giant yellow marigolds, groups of horses and cattle under clumps of great russet-and-black pine trees, range after range of distant hills, and the Three Brothers still pure white towering on the far skyline. It was a horse paradise: horses dozing in the early sun, and all horses full of good grass and fat. But inside two minutes, sixty wild horses were tearing over that range, squealing, kicking heels high in air, hoofs thundering. They knew what we were after — hide and seek, catch as catch can, a game played both on their side and on ours. It was past mid-day before (after some miracle) the seven horses we were after finally took the trail to the corral and we shut them in. Some time or other my hat had gone — I never noticed when.

*

Did you know that George, that wild-haired, red-faced bachelor of fifty, had once been engaged? It appears he had some lingering doubts, but the lady had him roped until they went out one day to Wolf Creek. She was a good horsewoman and rode one of George's best. When they started to come home she stuck in spurs and beat George back to Princeton by four miles over a hard road. George realized that a woman who would treat a horse like that was no wife for him.

Here's another horse touch. There was a man over to see Bert about a cow one evening and I went across the creek and joined them in the paddock. They were speaking of a man of over seventy, named Pigott. Two or three years ago a man came up all the way from the Yellowstone country near Wyoming with a band of cattle and some dandy saddle horses. He bought hay and wintered on the range near Princeton, stayed around all next summer doing nothing and left for parts unknown when Winter came again. The starving animals came down to Bert's ranch and he and George drove them back through snow to Pigott's place where there was plenty of hay. In the Spring Pigott figured that he owned the animals for the feed bill but he thought the horses "too good to sell." A day or two ago he rode into Princeton with his face all scratched up and it appeared that he had been bucked off into some bushes. "That is the the way I want to pass out," said he, "bucked onto my head off a real good horse." There is the real horseman's spirit!

This weekend Dart and I are going gipsying with our saddle horses and one pack-horse. We will camp out on the high range.

Yours ever,
Monnie

* * *

June 10, 1928
Dear Evie:

Two-forty-five in the afternoon and the telephone is ringing merrily like a kettle on the hob, but Miss Browning and I are going to try to get off something to remind you of the horse country that you will be back to in due course, in spite of interruptions.

*

The train had not yet whistled away up at Jura when the little Ford roared its way up the steep hill to Belfort Station yesterday afternoon.[15] Dart and Constance had come up to see me off, as well as George and Bert driving the car, so we sat in front of the little shed and looked over the beautiful rolling country below us with the Three Brothers, still splotched with snow, in the far distance.[16] Everything is green this year after Summer rains, and indescribably beautiful. When you walk or ride around, you are constantly getting little shocks from the beauty of the flowers, the contours of the hills, the little creeks, deer and what not.

As we sat there George, after taking a nap like some large animal, underneath a nearby tree, began to talk about bears. Years ago when he was young he remembered an old Indian telling him (with convincing detail) how there came one Winter a spell of terribly cold weather, something much worse than anything the old Indian had known. He was camped, could not keep warm and got scared as evening came on, so he went up the hills to a place that he knew of where there was a bear den and crawled in among the bears. He said they stirred and grunted a little in their sleep from time to time but did not wake up or take notice of him. When morning came he started for home.

George said you could tell a young bear's Winter home from an old one. Young bears would just scoop out a hole underneath a root or a log, but the old ones, learning every year by experience, would make themselves much more comfortable. They would pack in lots of dry grass and leaves and make themselves a nice nest. Sometimes when there would be untimely rains in the early Spring, some of the bears' dens would get wet and you would see them out looking for new quarters. He had sometimes poked a stick down into a black bear's den and got them to come out. In fact in mild weather they did not seem to be so dead asleep but would not stir when it was really cold, any more than the stiff little, almost frozen, chipmunks that you could sometimes find in their Winter nests in hollow logs. George had sometimes put dormant chipmunks near a fire and they would wake up after a bit, and play around in a sleepy sort of way.

The groundhogs den up for nearly six months, nice dry quarters with lots of good hay in them. Of course you know the bank beavers that make little stacks of well-cured hay and live on them in Winter time. George says they burrow down underneath the beds of creeks and then make an upraise (or whatever miners call it) to let the water in so that they have a way into the water and an outlet on land which makes them particularly safe when coyotes are prowling around or bears are hungry. When we were out with little Jean MacMillan the other day we saw many stones upturned by an old bear who lives back of Elephant Hill, on his hunt for grubs and ant eggs.[17] It must take a lot of these to make a meal, but the grass is good as a filler and there will be berries later on.

Two weeks ago Bert and George took a prominent citizen, Mr. X, up to the Summit with a lady cousin from Scotland who figured to be a horsewoman and insisted on riding a side saddle, which proved extremely unsuitable for the ups and downs of the high country. I had my horses out the same way and camped with them for company and also to give a little friendly help to Bert and George. Mr. X had not considered taking a cook and that end of the enterprise was suffering a little, both Bert and George being a little sketchy about meals as you know (for instance it is not everybody who likes to see his bacon on fire in a pan, which is part of the regular ritual of cooking as done by George), and table cloths look a little better when white, especially to the eyes of ladies straight from deer stalking in Scotland where there are footmen to hand things and the silver is not battered tin.

The trip was indescribably jolly up to the 5,500-foot level on Whipsaw Creek, but when we reached Cattle Camp near the Hope Summit and looked South towards the Nicomen, it was almost solid snow! The season up there was at least two weeks late. Desiring to show his woodsmanship, Mr. X selected a nice wet camp site, without dry wood, and it was quite a lot of work to make a comfortable camp. However, in the end Miss X had a lovely springy bed two feet deep in fir boughs. It looked rather romantic to be camped amongst all that snow. The horses stood around tied to trees, looking rather disconsolate since there was practically no feed — all except my two, Dixie and the little pack mare Edna. They and I had a cosy little camp by ourselves, under a spreading tree, with some nice oats for supper, blanketted against the cold wind. I did not bother to put up a tent.

Talk about horse intelligence — when I opened an eye next morning, Dixie, watching me, nickered at once. Then as I made no move towards the canvas nosebag that she uses, she reached forward, picked up a canvas pad which keeps the pack box away from Edna's ribs, and threw the pad at me. Still I did not move, so she got a canvas girth and threw it towards me. There were plenty of oats, so the hints worked.

That day we rode north along the Hope Summit to view the Skaist and mountain ranges beyond the Fraser River; also to visit an old pinto grizzly that George says lives up there. But the snow banks were deep and soft. It was nothing for George to slither down a steep slope and into soft snow level with the horse's back, and after various plungings get through to open ground beyond, but the lady from Scotland was scandalized at "such treatment of horses." It was an outrage, she said. Then George and I tried to explain that this was the only life and kind of movement these horses ever knew, that they were like cats upon their feet.

A distant fog came up and it was not warm. I must say the Summit country looked awful dreary, somewhat like the rocks and stunted shrubbery of Greenland must look on a dull day.

The side saddle irked the lady terribly, so I got on her horse and rode that way, while she took Dixie. Then we stopped and set fire to a clump of stunted Alpine trees which blazed like a furnace forty feet into the air, being very pitchy. The warmth and the cake I carried on the saddle cheered the party up a little but they had had enough and we went back to camp and dinner, later moving to a lower level and stopping the night at Powder Camp, which you remember last year.

I always tie Dixie and Edna with solid rope up to trees near my bedside so when, at one a.m., there was a great racket at the other camp and much stamping of horses' hoofs, I merely cocked an eye at the shadowy forms of my horses and went to sleep again. At three, when I got up, I fed my horses oats and thought to give them a few minutes grazing on the good grass near my little tent, so I turned them loose without trailing ropes and started cooking breakfast — coffee and oatmeal eaten straight. For a moment the porridge pot occupied my attention and when I looked round those horses had vanished into space. Me with my damaged feet!

So porridge pot and spoon in hand, I walked over to the other camp and here (3:30 a.m.) Bert was getting up and George's blankets were empty. "Did you hear the racket in the night?" asked Bert. "About one o'clock a chewing noise near my ear woke me up and there was a big old porcupine eating at our rawhide pack bags. I shooed him away and went back to bed. About five minutes later the chewing noise started again and there was the old fellow on the other side of the fire nibbling at the butt of my rifle. I got mad then and grabbed a stick and walloped him away. The noise woke some of the sleeping horses who, being just in off the range, are pretty scarey, and the first thing we knew there were loud snorts, the sound of tearing ropes, and a bunch of wild horses stampeding for the mountains. George has been after them all night."

"Well, I have lost mine too," said I.

On the trail towards Princeton, Bert and George had made a rope barricade with flaunting red blankets and a mile away George had put up regular wood bars five feet high, but the horses had bolted back to go the other way, and there was a big range to search for them. Bert and I found Dixie's hoof marks going straight up a slope that, from below, looked like the side of this Metropolitan Building and about three times as high. In searching for their trail I had by this time eaten the porridge. When, very blown in the wind, we reached the high grazing lands, I used the pot and spoon as a sort of bell to attract Dixie's attention. However they made no bones about it and we led them back to camp quite happily. Enough horses were salvaged to take Mr. and Miss X into Princeton, but Bert surely did have a mountain of suitcases, pack boxes and blanket rolls on the one pack-horse! At Nine-Mile Creek the little Ford met us, Bert turned back to help George hunt the missing horses, and I went on into town riding Edna, leading Dixie and Monty, with Silver skirmishing around behind us. Dixie by this time had lost three shoes. You know the appalling way they fix on old shoes or forget to shoe the horses. I make a point now of taking the horses we use down to the smith regularly.

Dart and Constance have been spending ten days at our shack in that lovely grove of trees just across the little creek from Bert's ranch house. There are always a raft of children around Mrs. Thomas, her own and others who come and go indefinitely. They had twenty-two grownups and children at the mid-day meal last Sunday and Heaven knows how many slept in or around the house. I do not know how many beds there are, but there must be plenty of blankets. They are the most united family we have ever met, so kind and considerate of each other, never the least hint of ill-temper or dispute. Bert is so easy-going himself, and anything goes with Mrs. Thomas.

Of course, it is what the tidy would call a hugger-mugger. Dogs worry sitting ducks until their frenzied quackings bring Dart or Constance running from across the creek; cabbage plantings wither because somebody has forgotten to turn the water on; the Ford goes to town without the tub of cream that should be shipped to Grand Forks; the Skyline camping equipment is a mere heap on a barn floor; somebody has borrowed the shoeing tools and has not returned them, so a shoe is hammered on somehow or other without them; the horses that should be in have broken through a fence and are ten miles away somewhere; there is the white turkey somewhere out in the alfalfa fields desperately surrounded by crows, but nobody remembers to go and look for it; and so on and so on! But all as happy as they can be with an unconscious sound philosophy that nothing matters enough to be worth worry.

I am inclined to think that, like George, these people are amongst the successful, though Heaven knows what their annual turnover in dollars can be. Both Bert and George are free from the dollar taint — for instance I find Bert has just taken $35 for a trip he made in connection with a timber matter when we should have paid him $65, and he and George asked $50 instead of $112 from Mr. X because they felt the lateness of the Summit season had spoiled the trip.

Here is some campfire talk that stuck in my mind — Mr. X fresh from a trip to New Zealand, telling about the Maori who figured he was partly Scotch. "We Maori people," he said, "believe in transmigration of souls and my ancestors have eaten many Scotchmen." Then there was the story of the Los Angeles man who died and went to the Golden Gate — St. Peter said, "Well, you can come in but you won't like it here." Someone was reminded of the Chicago citizen who died and was being shown over the arrangements in the next world. "Even after Chicago," he said, "I had no notion that Heaven was such a fine place." "Well," said his guide, "this isn't *Heaven* you know." But Miss X was not quite happy in her human contact. She referred to Bert and George as "the men" in quite the wrong way. You know what fine people they are.

When Jean and Mrs. MacMillan were up last week I woke Jean and George for breakfast at 4 a.m. It was not until we were viewing that wide country from the high summit of the Elephant some hours later that I remembered leaving all the breakfast food spread on the grass beside my tent and I remembered that Phyllis Thomas has a new large puppy dog. There was no dog seen that day, nor one large cake, one brown loaf, one pitcher milk, one-half pot porridge, one-half pound butter in aluminum screw-top tin, also missing. One dog sleeping it off somewhere. Accidents like this, Monty busting my new bridle at the shoesmith's, the upsetting of a tin of powdered milk among my clothes all gooey since, the fishing-rod left behind at a camp ground, and so on and so on, these are inevitable incidents.

You would like the birds that are nesting near our shack door — birds of dazzling bright blue; and the little baby grouse that George's marvellous sight alone could distinguish from the surrounding ground; and those beautiful mule deer standing close by at graze, then gliding away in their effortless bounding movement. There is a hen grouse near George's shack that comes off the nest at 8 p.m. sharp, receives a little grain thrown out by one of George's irrigation Chinamen (he has two working his ranch on half shares), exercises for fifteen minutes by the clock and goes back to her eggs. The old beaver up the creek is rebuilding his damaged dam. Dart watched a duck with 11 young ones in trouble in the rough waters of the creek until the tears came into her eyes, she said. It was an awfully affecting sight.

Little boy Evan has collected sixty dozen empty beer bottles from One-Mile Road, sold them for 20 cents a dozen and bought a bicyle. We have given him all the unnecessary items of our equipment, which he will trade with other boys for Heaven knows what. He earned a suit of clothes helping to build our shack — at least he got the money and bought clothes. Twelve years old!

There was one thing that the lady from Scotland did admire and that was the good breeding of Bert's and George's horses. She said they would fetch good prices in the Old Country. It is rather sad to think that they alone of all the old-timers in that Interior country have remained faithful to the horse tradition in these days of smelly gasoline.

Here is George's story about Whitey, who as you know is a perfectly reasonable horse. Young Morton (whoever he is) is rather bullying with horses and when he mounted Whitey one time, Whitey instantly bucked him off. They wondered what was the matter and Morton tried again with the same result, so one of the girls got on Whitey and all was well; then two of the girls got on Whitey together and nothing happened; then young Morton tried again and Whitey lay down and rolled over with his feet in the air just like a dog. He did not intend to let young Morton ride him. Boy is much the same — he will buck off anyone he does not like and even kick at him, but is perfectly charming to his friends.

So I left that heavenly country yesterday evening, snoozing all the way in the train, and here Miss Browning has had her afternoon wrecked while we get these notes to you — there goes the phone ...

Ever your affectionate uncle

Chapter Three
WITH HORSES in the WEST

When people ask me, "Do you go alone into that wilderness?" I always say, "Oh no, there are four of us." Besides myself there is the big mare, the little mare and Buck. I am no horseman — I merely sit upon horses, in an elderly way. So you must understand that Buck is merely short for buckskin (the colour of tanned hide) and that all my horses are gentle with me, though they fight spiritedly among themselves at times. Their home is on the slopes of Five-Mile Range not far from a small farming settlement in the Cascade Mountains, and when I am down in civilization attending to my business they have a good time there, browsing on good bunch grass, mixing in local horse society, dozing in groups underneath the trees. Even in Winter, thanks to my business, they do themselves well while their friends have to rustle (which means paw snow to reach dried grass) and stand 30 or 40 degrees below zero in the open.

There are roads in these mountain valleys and nearly all the ranchers, even the Indians, have cars. The money that used to circulate in the district and make it prosperous when everyone rode or drove horses, and hay and grain were raised to feed them — this money now drains away to the outside world in payment for second-hand cars and petrol. The young folks have no use for horses. They move only in cars or trucks, even to fetch a load of hay or to go 200 yards from house to barn. So horses are no longer bred, as mine were, from part Thoroughbred stock. It is very difficult to get good animals. "When the Bar-X cattle were moving to their summer range," an ex-cowboy friend of mine told me the other day, "I met the herd of spare horses for the riders that is driven with them; measly scrubs, it made my heart ache, remembering the old days."

Here and there, as with my friend, the Western spirit still survives. I rode over the hills early one morning to see old man Pigott, he who at different times has had almost every bone broken by horses; he who was bucked into a thorn bush last Fall by a vivid young thing and (after a drink or two) proudly said, "That's how I want to pass out, boys — bucked off a real good horse." When I reached the fine high corral alongside Pigott's log house, old Bill Owen was milking there. "Where's Pigott?" I asked. "He's still here," said Bill grinning, "but it's my belief he damn near passed out just before midnight. Did you hear he got hurt again Tuesday?" I found Pigott sitting on the edge of his bunk, fully dressed, seventy-seven years old, three ribs broken (that the doctor had set). "Something busted in my shoulder," he said. Go to hospital he would not; he "was in one once for fifteen days. That's enough." There are nearly a hundred head of his horses wandering around on Five-Mile and other ranges; most of them, in his opinion, too good to sell. Nice stock they are, but too high-life for most people.

Buck Wilson is another survivor of the past. Buck's business is prospecting, which means getting someone to put up a summer's supply of bacon, beans, flour, sugar and coffee and going off into the mountains with a partner and half a dozen horses. Nothing whatever happens, in the way of mineral discovery, but Buck and the partner and the horses live the life they love and optimism springs eternal. Once, away off in the solitudes, I found an old grandpapa frying fish at the door of his little tent, alongside a creek, his two hobbled horses grazing nearby. Western born, he was, and his father before him. "When I was a boy," he quavered, "there was a prospector from these hills comed to our house with a bit of rock and him and father roasted it in the kitchen stove and got a bead of gold out of it. I'm going to find the place that rock comed from, I am."

There is an old-timer who has copper claims and a log cabin in which he lives, thirty miles from anywhere, over rugged mountain trails. I heard the tinkle of his horsebells one evening and rode downhill to camp with him. We discussed a rumour that a new transcontinental highway might pass that way. "If they build a road into here and buy my claims," he said sadly, "where am I to go?" I felt much the same about it, myself. Too much of the world's surface is infested with cars, and people.

After the turmoil of city business, these old-timers of the mountain country are very restful. They have almost no money, no urge to get it, no tension. They have more freedom than most rich people. Round a campfire one said, "What beats me is the way you city folk fuss yourselves. Slaving away for more and more money. What's the idea?" Of course when illness comes, or crippling accident, these people are out of luck; like their horses or the deer, they may die without a doctor.

*

One vital need is that one's pack-horse should lead intelligently — should understand what a pull on the lead rope means; use sense in choosing which side of a tree to pass; not get hysterical if the rope gets between its legs. My left arm was almost crippled for two months because Edna, small-brained like a frog, had a way of stopping dead during a trot; whereupon the lead rope would rip through my grip and often, before Dixie would rein up, the strain of holding to the rope-end would catch my elbow with a jolt. Once my thumb caught in a snarl of the rope and hung me between the two horses. Then I changed to easy-going old Skidoo, who proved even worse with his hostility to any gait other than the one he wanted, so that I had to hitch the rope around the saddle bow and let Dixie jerk his jaw every few minutes, mile after mile. Every trick of leading that I know proved vain, and it made exasperation worse to know that any loss of temper would be fatal. Friendly feeling between the three of us makes all the difference in these trips. Afterwards Bert remembered a cowboy dodge of passing the rope just behind the ears where, it appears, there is a tender spot, pressure on which starts a horse forward instantly.

However, on my Bank Holiday trip with Eve no such urge was needed. As Dixie trotted or covered ground in her fast striding walk, the little mare kept up behind, the lead rope coming in or paying out through my hands with a sort of pleasant rhythm, rope and reins exercising one's arms while leg and body muscles did centaur work in the continual ups and downs of rough ground; all very restful to one's mind, which is apt to ruminate aimlessly by the hour over some new idea in camping kit or such-like simple thing. A fine escape from business thinking.

The horse and I had had a heavy day, climbing and descending ridge after ridge that crossed our way. At 5 p.m. I was still intending to camp in lower country beside some creek, but as we topped the last high ridge, Dixie, famished, began fighting the reins to bite at tufts of grass. A clump of stunted Alpine trees offered a campsite, and the view of nine mountain ranges, row upon row, seen violet in a slight haze of forest-fire smoke, was enthralling. I had a little water in my bag so I stopped right there.

I was not warm; not an air stirred; no rustling of water came from any creek; no bird called. From where she grazed nearby not even the crunching of Dixie's teeth could be heard. When, in case of storm, I had chopped out stables for the horses in the thicket made by three trees and made a lying place for myself, the mountain silence came down upon us dead. Big Dixie went on eating — nothing ever bothers her — but the little pack mare shifted uneasily, turned her head this way and that with pricked ears, nose in air. She sniffed and every now and then gave a snort of fear. Ghosts or the distant smell of some wild animal? After a while my scalp would tighten and a little cold thrill run down my spine at each snort. Edna was used to being with a mob of horses down below in gentle country. She had known Dixie and myself very little before this trip. Isolation amid high rugged scenery worried her. To make a homely noise I put a bell on Dixie. The little mare began to eat.

I lit a small fire and toasted the wholewheat bread that, with warm water, made my supper. The stars came out bigger and more brilliant than when seen from lower country. I sat in my shirtsleeves brooding over space and stars and dark

With Horses in the West

looming stupendous mountains, with a lump in my throat at the magnificence of it all. All I remembered of the agitated city life 100 miles away and far below shrivelled to pinpoint size. That is one reason why I make these mountain trips, it cools one's mind.

People who go up high in parties do not get this uplift of the mind. It was not lonesome — two friendly horses were nearby. And when the red ball of the full moon rose suddenly behind a distant ridge, I turned into my quilt-and-canvas bed very comfortably.

As you know I can walk very little, so in the mountains I take no risk of losing horses. If they should get away, what could I do but sit and wait on short rations until a search party should come? So I have a heavy leather strap, six feet long, that buckles to a foreleg of each horse and is attached to 40 feet of rope. If a horse gets tangled up during the night the leather will not cut its fetlocks as would the rope. Hobble, strap and rope for two horses weigh eight pounds; bells, nosebags, hand axe and odds and ends make up another six; feather quilt, canvas cover, sheepskin and tentlet, total another twelve; for my food, say eight pounds; oats for a three-day trip say 25; sixty pounds in all — a bagatelle for a sturdy horse.

I take pleasure in simplified meals. One meal is rolled oats boiled with a little butter; another is a chunk of cooked meat that keeps perfectly in that pure high air. Another meal is raisins, another wholewheat toast and butter, and water with the chill off with each meal. Hunger dictates which kind of meal is next, and three of the four can be eaten as one rides by merely opening a holster with one hand while reins and leading rope are held in the other, and one's heels guide the saddle horse onward. My potlets assembled from the 15-cent store weigh a total of four ounces, a fine instance of "one's money's worth." They do the work well. How more soul-satisfying these things are than the clumsy heavy expensive things the outfitters make. Such simplicity gives me a sense of confident independence. I cease to feel daunted by other people's wealth as I do in town amid the big cars and luxuries. That is another reason for these trips. What does it matter anyhow if so many inestimable persons are getting richer than oneself? In ten or twenty years or so ...!

*

Nine grub sacks and bundles went with us on Friday evening. Bob met us at Belfort and we had breakfast at the shack at 5 a.m. Then there was a great spreading out of two weeks' supplies:

For food: A cooked chicken, roast beef, ham, canned fruit, milk, rice, bread, rolled oats, coffee, cocoa, oranges, lime juice, carrots, onions, marmalade, honey, jam, prunes, figs, chocolates, eggs.

For camp stuff: A seven-pound silk tent, my wife's thin rollup mattress, jaegar blanket, sheepskin, eiderdown, rainproof canvas coverlet, my ground sheet, small eiderdown, sheepskin, canvas cover and sleeping helmet, mosquito tents, nest of aluminum pots and kitchen stuff, waterbag, canvas bucket.

For the horses: Saddles, bridles, halters, tie ropes, hobbles, pack saddles, 40-foot-long pack ropes, saddle blankets, pads, packboxes, manteaus, saddle bags, oats for catching horses.

Miscellaneous articles: A game-getter (combination small rifle and shotgun), pocket fishing-rod, fish net (illegal), axe, file, stove, pocket tool set, bits of rope, string, tape, thongs, rivets, copper wire, a few nails, slivers of pitchy wood to kindle wet weather fires, cotton bags, writing paper, notebook, a map, compass, waterproof matchbox, soap, towels, candles, hospital kit, camera, gun oil, collapsible rubber bath, safety pins.

Various clothes: Raincoats, thick frieze coats, sweaters, mosquito nets, spare garments, buckskin gloves, puttees, etc.

Believe me, it took some time and work to put all these things in suitable bags and tins, to roll them up or tie them, to stow them so that the pack for each side of a horse would weigh the same. And the horses themselves were hard to catch that morning. Little boy Evan caught the two pack-horses, Edna and Skidoo, and took them into Princeton to the shoesmith. Finally, after being on the go since 5 a.m., I started from the ranch myself at 6 p.m., riding Dixie and leading Monty packed with only my own bedding. At Princeton I stopped for a good supper in a restaurant while the horses filled up on hay at a livery stable.

Then, the one main street being cluttered with Saturday night's assemblage of motor cars, cowboys in for the July Bank Holiday sports, dogs, children and drunk miners, I worked my way by back streets out of town and uphill on Nine-Mile Road. Not easily either, for Monty resented being tied to Skid's tail, in the manner usual when one man has a string of horses to lead, and he reared up at intervals and made Skid annoyed about the roots of his tail. Edna kept stopping dead, forefeet spread firm, doing this suddenly with a jolt that would jar every joint in my left arm, and after I had loosed Monty and was leading him with a long third rope, this kept getting between someone else's forelegs, much to everyone's concern. We criss-crossed the road and got mixed up around roadside trees at first. Then I tied Skid to Monty's pack and all was well for some distance, except for the jolt from Edna at every side trail which she wished to turn into. Then the tie rope got under Monty's pack and made him plunge a bit and it got between Skid's foreleg and Edna broke away several times. All this in the dark, with the road ahead just showing dimly, meant slow going and warm work. It was 20 minutes to twelve when I reachd Nine-Mile camp and tied the horses up. Then I saw that Dart's saddle blanket and hair pad had slipped from under Edna's saddle and gone.

In the darkness at Nine-Mile it took me a solid hour to climb up and down the steep sidehill and tether out the horses in suitable spots (good feed and no obstacles they could wind themselves round), each with a hobble on one foreleg, a six-foot leather strap attached to the hobble (so that the horses would not get their legs burned with rope if they should get tangled up), and then forty feet of tie rope to a stake or tree.

Just as I was finishing, along came a motor car going to the coal mine up Nine-Mile Creek. I hollered but they didn't hear. Figuring that they must have seen my lost horse blanket and hair pad, I slipped a bridle on Skid and followed them. It was pitch dark in the deep narrow defile of Nine-Mile and Skid went very slow, nor could I urge him very vigorously, riding bareback on the deep-rutted, soggy, rocky road that seemed to be underfoot. After ages, I glimpsed some camp buildings and a car alongside the road. Reaching into the car my hand touched the hair pad on the driver's seat, but no blanket. I got back to camp at twenty-to-two, laughing at how the car owner would be puzzled next morning to miss that good hair pad. So to bed under a tree for a very short nap.

*

Since noon today my wife and I have been loafing just below the summit of the high range north of Hope Pass, looking at the gorgeous view. Mosquitoes were pestiferous when we came — I would like the manufacturer of the netting we put up to see the way they crawled through his miserable product. Dart tried reading — and gave it up. I lay on the other side of a tree with my netting scarf draped over a pack saddle and tried to read and doze. "Heavens," we said suddenly, "why haven't we made a smudge?" — and now that three little mounds are spreading smoke into the surrounding air, the burning feel of mosquito bites has ceased, and profound and grateful peace has come upon the World. As I write, Skidoo and Monty doze within six feet of me standing in the smoke; Dixie is lying down in the lush grass nearby — too full to eat. Edna still nibbles at the end of her tie rope. We came up here this morning from our camp to give the horses a picnic on the high range grass and they have surely had it. Edna carried our pack — waterbag, coffee-pot, grub, the aforesaid netting, coats and a rug to lie on, hobbles and drag ropes for three horses. Edna has to be led; Skidoo knows his job and comes along unbidden, a wise old horse.

In our party of six, my wife and I and the four horses, we get to know each other very well. Dixie is of course boss horse — big handsome Dixie with the grand manner, who keeps the others in their dependent places; Monty and Skid, who are everybody's friends; and sturdy little small-brained Edna, who might play the part of kitchen maid to Dixie's Duchess.

The first three understand people, use their heads, have obvious intelligence. Edna is in a state of startled stupidity at every human action. Count upon Edna to tangle herself up in tie ropes, snort at the witness of a cloth, tremble at the rustle of a canvas pack cover. Just because Bert and George and Lafon had camped with us before, our horses had been driven up to range with theirs that night on the good grass around Twin Lakes. Getting free by accident some days afterwards, Edna deliberately left our tethered three and headed up the Twin Lakes trail at a rapid trot. Obviously she thought that our friends' horses were still there. Dixie and the others knew by observation that Bert and his bunch had gone over the hills northward, and they would never dream of leaving their own party and going solitary in that way.

Mabel "Dart" Grainger, left, and Martin Grainger at the Thomas ranch, June 1928. (COURTESY BC ARCHIVES AND RECORDS SERVICE)

Chapter Four
LETTERS, 1929

July 10, 1929
Dear Mr. Denny:

On Friday evening I found myself on the Canadian National train with a party of twelve young bloods of Vancouver and Percy Williams, the famous Canadian sprinter and world's champion, quite a nice unspoiled boy.[18] In the smoking room of the train the bloods immediately called for *appollonaris* and produced whisky, which led to one of them calling for a survey of resources. It then appeared there were among the party nineteen bottles of whisky and six of gin and it was hurriedly resolved to remedy this shortage by securing another dozen bottles at Ashcroft, which we would reach in the early morning.

Ashcroft is a charming little village on the banks of the North Thompson River with the big bare hills of the Dry Belt behind it. Motor cars awaited us and we drove some sixty miles up the Old Cariboo Highway over which so many gold-seekers passed when the famous rush was on in the sixties. We stopped at one or two hamlets en route in order to go through various ceremonies with the bottles and everybody was feeling nicely invigorated by the time we branched off into the deep ruts of a country road which led over a further ten miles to Green Lake, where the rodeo was to be. Perhaps I should say that my own invigoration came from the air and sun and scenery rather than the other source.

That country is a high plateau, four thousand feet elevation, full of little lakes, a grass country with thickets of little aspens and a few larger trees — always charming in the early summer greenery. The race course was the grass and dusty track of the roadway. Between it and the lake there was a fringe of little trees under which people camped in tents or automobile trucks or just under the sky — with motor cars, old-fashioned horse vehicles, saddle horses tied to trees, horses wandering about, Indians in enormous hats and high-heeled boots, Indian women in blazing colours, green, yellow and scarlet, Indian children and dogs — all most picturesque under the bright blue sky with the turquoise of the pretty lake seen through the trees. On the other side of the road was a fenced-in field where the bucking horses would perform; further up the road was a large barn for a dance hall, some tent restaurants, a hot-dog stand, a card game, canvas stables for the racing horses, Indian families in camp, more horses, more dogs.

After mid-day dinner a local rancher, Jack Boyd, master of the ceremonies, with an enormous hat and megaphone, announced the first race, which took place in a cloud of dust, and then race after race, all keenly contested, Indians and white men, local people on local horses, and good fun. There must have been other bottles there besides those of our party, for after the fourth race a well-intoxicated half-breed gentleman came up to accuse Jack Boyd of an unfair decision, whereupon Jack knocked him down with the megaphone and a lively scrap took place full in the public view. Unfortunately, there were two provincial police there on the outlook for bootleggers and they interfered before a decision was reached, but it was a good fight while it lasted. Then, as if nothing had happened, Boyd proceeded with the next race and so on, until we all moved down to the fenced field for the rougher sports.

In the neighbouring grasslands between the thickets of trees, mounted men had been herding a band of wild cattle. Another group were herding a bunch of wild horses and these were urged gradually into runways which had narrow ends into which one animal at a time could be pocketed. Then if it was a wild horse a saddle would be lowered onto its back and the girths (by some legerdemain) buckled by men reaching their hands in through the confining bars. When the saddle was ready the rough-rider would climb over the bars and drop down on top of the horse, whereupon the men outside would open the gate and out would dash a frenzied animal with a cowboy swaying on top, whooping and yelling and flapping his enormous hat against the horse's flanks.

Some of the cowboys were drunk and some were sober, some of them stuck on and some turned double somersaults and came down smack with breath-taking narrow escapes when the horses would kick at them wildly as they fell. Wild steers came out with simply a rope around them to which a rider held, usually for a few brief moments only. Then there were wild cows to be roped and milked, and wild calves to be roped and tied up, and steers to be caught by the horns by cowboy wrestlers and thrown to the ground. One Indian had come from another rodeo a week before with his right arm dangling from some collar-bone injury, but I saw him ride two bucking horses and he was thrown twice from the backs of wild steers.

One of the wild horses broke through the fence and made off through the timber, bucking as he went, his rider having nothing but a rope halter to guide him. They sent out a search party which ultimately found the man thrown between two tree stumps, unconscious, with his chest all bruised — but I noticed him dancing that evening. By supper time quite a proportion of the people one saw had limps, but they all seemed to feel good and all were present till 4 a.m. at the dance hall, except when they went out to have a drink. There was no unpleasant drunkenness, however, and one gained a tremendous respect for the pluck and physical toughness which these people had. It made me feel very old to think I would not dream of exposing myself to such vicissitudes.

The next day's sports were much the same, but that evening they danced right through the night till eight o'clock next morning. I spent a good part of the night watching them, for it was really quite a festive spectacle — some five hundred people dancing in the way that we remember forty years ago — country dancing with rhythmic stamping on the floor and gallops and a great deal of vigorous movement. About two o'clock I thought of my blankets underneath a tree and went there and lit a fire at which I sat watching the brilliant stars. After an hour the dawn began to show in the Northern sky and it seemed a shame to go to bed so I watched the sky and the lake and the dancing alternately until breakfast time at four o'clock.

At the restaurant the poor Swedish couple running it were nearly dead with fatigue, so I amused myself for an hour and a half washing up three hundred plates and cups and saucers in extremely dirty water (there being no one to fetch clean water) until my action began to produce a domestic crisis. The old couple were straight Swede peasantry but there were asleep (after a night's dancing) on a mattress thrown on the ground just beyond the open-air stove, the younger generation, two well-dressed girls who would have passed muster in a smart city office, plus a young man who seemed to be more or less engaged to one of them. Papa shifted the daughters with his foot and pointed to me, so I went and had my breakfast for which they refused to take any payment. Then I sat for hours watching the Indian familes pack up and go, and the half-breed and white cowboys with their bright scarves, championship belts, and all kinds of horses wandering around being saddled, the whole thing just like a moving picture show.

Afterwards, driving back to Ashcroft we all fell asleep, and so back to Vancouver. It was a real country festival.

* * *

September 18, 1929
Dear Mr. Denny:

With hands all grime and scratches, and black and broken nails, in sweater, dirty shirt open at the neck, patched stained riding breeches freshly torn at the knee, and ragged canvas shoes; with every muscle stiff from fatigue — a would-be philosopher sat by a train window watching the mountain gorge through which a railroad was carrying him back to hot water and soap, city clothes and business. For some hours he had time to spare, so he took pencil and pad and wrote this letter.

*

My mountain folk have very little money and even less keenness to earn it. There is something baffling about them; after all these years I can't quite understand how their minds work. For there are times when they certainly need money — in illness for instance, when trips must be made to Vancouver, to the hospital. An impatient city friend of mine says it is just as if they all had hookworm (the parasite said to make the poor whites in the Southern states so shiftless). I myself think their lack of "get up" is caused by something missing in their diet, for they live mostly upon potatoes, white bread and rice pudding with meat once a week and a few eggs and milk. No green vegetables or fruit; no variety.

Around a campfire, however, my friend Bert will sometimes open up and argue the point. "Why worry about money the way you city people do?" he will ask. "As long as a fellow can see his way a month or two ahead, what does it matter? Why bother with all those luxuries? You people haven't any time to enjoy them anyway. Here we're all good-tempered and easy-going and happy. What more should we get by fussing ourselves?" After being heated up all week in meetings and offices and clubs where men's thoughts seem focussed upon the dollar hunt and the word dollar occurs in almost every spoken sentence, I find it very tranquillizing to drop suddenly into a mountain world where money means so little. Especially if I'm still mourning over dollars that "might have been" but for some error of judgment.

*

This time when I reached the mountains and got off the train at 5 a.m., I walked first downhill to see if the new fence was finished. Three months it was since some horses had pushed over the old one, and Bert had had one good horse crippled in the wire and my big chestnut narrowly escaped, with a six-inch gash in his fetlock. It made me so angry at the time that Bert had promised to get the fence fixed "right away." So in a week or two Roy Martin took a contract to do it and worked two days. Then he had to get his hay in; then he went haying for a neighbour; then, two weeks running, he promised faithfully to begin next Monday. Finally, in another loss of temper I rode into Princeton, hired two men myself, bought them provisions, lent them a tent, delivered them in a car upon the job at 6 a.m., and hoped for results before any more horses should be damaged.

Well, in a week, I could see that the two men had done as much as you and I, in our younger days, would have accomplished in a day and a half. However, the fence would plainly be finished some time; and that, for Arcadia, was satisfactory. So I walked on to my shack where five hungry horses whinnied welcome to me, the King of Oats. They never see oats except when I'm there. I'm riotously popular.

*

A trip with three horses, one led, one following loose, sounds fine, but it did not work this time. The two big ones have been bullying Ribbons, the cob, and he followed us without enthusiasm. When bands of horses crossed the road he would dash madly after them; reach a high hill and whinny distractedly, looking now at me below, now at the wild horses, torn between conscience and freedom. I'd whinny back and call "Come little horse" and he'd charge downhill, head down, heels in the air, in high spirits, much to the jeopardy of the pack he carried. Then he would stop and graze, with much distant calling from me, who feared he would forget the rest of us and turn back home. It was such slow travelling that 16 miles out I changed over, letting the big chestnut loose. He, I knew, was touchingly devoted to the mare I was riding and would presumably follow her in country he had never seen before.

As he felt the rope loosen, the chestnut looked at me and tossed his head. If a horse can smile that horse smiled. Then, in a quiet gentlemanly way, he turned around and trotted homeward down the trail. Since there was nothing else that could be done, the rest of us followed meekly after. So for twelve miles we travelled back to Princeton, my chief preoccupation being to keep the chestnut from hurrying himself, for when he galloped he shifted his pack (which was getting very loose) and the more he did that the more chance there was that it would slip round underneath his body, whereupon, in the approved manner of such occasions, he would probably kick it to bits. My precious pack!

I had lots of time to be pleased with several things. Firstly it was a fine sunny day and a pleasure to be alive in that good air and in such charming surroundings. The interrupted trip did not matter, it was just as good exercise and occupation following that horse. Secondly, I was glad to feel no trace of temper. Some people shout at horses and jerk at their bits and hit them and lose their tempers. Now that I live with horses so much I never do any of these things. Why not the same quiet courtesy between man and horses as between gentlemen of the old school? They detest noise and sudden shocks of any kind, they are sensitive to fine shades of behaviour. Why spoil that? Living with them you learn how much thought can be exchanged without spoken language. "Gentle" horses would never dream of hurting a human being and even their kickings of each other are not meant viciously. The other day I intercepted a short-leg kick that Dixie intended for her friend the big chestnut. It caught me on the fleshy part of the thigh — brrump! like a shell exploding — but afterwards I realized that it had not hurt and was merely a lady's gesture of impatience at being kept waiting, tied to a tree.

The third thing that pleased me was the manner in which that chestnut picked out the exact way that we had come from home. He had come from California and had never been on the Skyline Trail until that morning. There were conflicting trails going in every direction. I have my own particular bridle paths with special little cut-offs that I like to take — and that chestnut never failed to take the exact path, the exact cut-off, the exact detour round a fallen tree, that I had taken coming out. How did he do it? He must have had those twelve miles of country photographed in his mind like a cinema reel. Partly, I think, by scent, for he would snuff the ground at times. They tell me that if you carry a dog in an airtight box into which no smells of passing country can penetrate, he will be unable to

Letters, 1929

Along the Skyline Trail, Martin Grainger in front. (COURTESY BC ARCHIVES AND RECORDS SERVICE)

find his way home any distance, but if his nose is free he will map by smell.

Well, I caught Mr. Coat, the chestnut, in the main street of the little town just before his pack came off. There had been widespread forest fires on Copper Montain where the mines are and the firefighters were all in to get their pay. By happy coincidence the long-closed beer parlours were to open that afternoon by Government permission. So there were soon lively times in Princeton. Even at fourscore years the whitehaired watchman at the local sawmill had his scalp split by a beer bottle later in the day. As for myself, travelling with three horses seemed too slow. I went back to my shack, cooked a good meal and made ready for a fresh start early next morning. Bert came down from the hills where he is bossing some Government trail cutting and I told him about Henry.

*

Henry McDiarmid was a quiet man, soft spoken and unobtrusive. He had a large family — of nine children I think — and worked hard underground in a job at the copper mine. Then his health gave way, indigestion leading to stomach ulcers, and he went out on the hills to earn money as a fire warden. I remember coming down the valley of Roche River on one of my lonely trips this Summer and finding Henry's camp — just a bed of pine boughs on the ground, a bind of hewn wood high on stilts to protect his cache of food from wild animals, and a box nailed to a tree alongside the trail wherein Henry had left a scrawl setting forth his whereabouts. I had rolled a couple of cigars (which I carry for such purposes) in an old telegram that I found in my pocket, and was leaving them in the box by way of a visiting card when Henry and his horses came in from a trip.

We sat and talked about the open-air life and about the wild things and good places for horsefeed and all that sort of thing. Henry never said a word of complaint, though he must have been feeling pretty ill. He doubted what doctors could do for him. He had the pressing urgency of earning money for wife and nine children, and Henry had looked the situation in the face and figured he would stick it out.

A few weeks later the constant pain of riding got him. He awoke from a faint to find himself fallen from his horse and lying upon a trail. It took him four hours of desperate effort to crawl a mile to an old cabin where, by some astounding luck, old Charlie Bonafia discovered him. I saw Henry in hospital, wasted and uncomplaining, not long before he died. It may have been bad judgment, it may have been futile (as people said) for him to have carried on until it was too late. Something about it, however, caught me by the throat — a glimpse of the heroic such as one sometimes had as a boy in Greek and Roman stories or those Icelandic sagas.

*

By star and fire light next morning I fed the horses and myself and saddled up and packed. "Travel light" is the motto for happiness on camping trips just as it should be in Life, but it has taken me years of error to get rid of the unnecessary. Do you know what I take now? Here is the list:

Lbs.
20 oats (for a three or four day trip)
 4 picket rope with leather strap and hobble
 4 featherweight canvas nightgowns for two horses
14 eiderdown quilt; canvas cover; short warm coat for me
 1 hand axe
 8 bags of oatmeal, wholewheat loaf, butter, piece of meat or ham
 2 waterbags, tiny cooking pot, matches, string, scarf, iodine, bandages, candle, compass, spoon
— Total: 53 lbs.

Upon the saddle add raincoat and sweater, tie ropes for the horses and a second loaf of bread for emergency eating. In cold weather add warm gloves and extra socks to pull over one's shoes when riding.

I feel that Marcus Aurelius and his Stoic friends would approve this set-up, but none of my acquaintances have seemed to want to go with me. Another objection they might have would be the hours. Down Town we are slaves of Time, set duties at set hours, set meals, hurrying all day to catch up with Time. In the mountains Time has ceased to be except when I look at my watch on the last morning to see how many hours separate me from Princeton and the Vancouver train at 3 p.m. Bedtime is when it is too dark to see; time to get up is when I wake in the small hours before dawn; mealtimes are when hunger dictates or when there is good grass for horsefeed. A meal is either oatmeal boiled with butter, or wholewheat bread, or a piece of meat, whichever is the most convenient or attractive at the time. And we travel during all the hours of light except when the horses get too hungry and insist on oating. With so light a pack each horse is practically resting half the time, for I change from one to the other, for riding, every three hours.

Well, this time I took two horses and went into lower country following a pretty little winding creek valley for twenty miles or so, and then branching off into the hills that lead north towards the big cattle ranch at Douglas Lake. Toward late afternoon the weather changed and about 7 p.m., when camp and supper and rest were three thoughts that filled our minds, there came a sudden blast of wind and cataracts of rain. The storm caught us high on an exposed hillside; away below there were trees and a fenced enclosure, and we beat our way gradually downhill, wet and dishevelled.

There was a settler in a cabin who called to me to come indoors, but I hate houses when I can escape them and so made camp beneath three trees that kept the worst of the downpour away. Later I paid my formal visit to the cabin, admired the usual bits of copper-stained rock that every prospector has upon his table, talked mining and cattle and fishing and horses with my host, heard anecdotes of the early days, agreed that a certain amount of ash and cinders in food was good for any man, and that an open-air life was the only proper one, while wondering "how them fellers can stick it down in them blank blank cities;" and so said goodnight and fared into the dark again, falling into an irrigation ditch on my way to camp and finding two very discontented horses, unable to sleep for wet, and pawing great holes at the foot of the trees to which I had tied them.

Going to bed is easy for me. Usually I poke my shod feet into a thin canvas bag (to protect the quilt) put my coat for a pillow and roll into the eiderdown, pulling the canvas cover over me, with saddlery and packs grouped around my head. With horses, an emergency may come up at any moment in the night, especially when one is far off in the high Summit country. A horse may get loose or be tangled in its tie rope or get scared at some wild animal (even a porcupine can raise a riot in the dark). Then one has to spring up literally *cap a pie* and ready for action. After a few experiences of stumbling over rocks and tree limbs in stockinged feet in the dark, I am solid for shoes on in bed, depraved as it may sound. But on this particular evening (being so wet) I took a chance and indulged in the luxury of taking them off.

*

We were on our way home next morning long before the settler awoke. Both horses were hungry and fed up with being wet. The pace kept increasing. We swooped down hillsides and tried to gallop along the flats with wet bushes on either side of the trail slapping us with spray. After a while the big chestnut went ahead, pulling hard upon the lead rope, and there was I, a sort of human gearshift stretched between two highly powered engines and working desperately to and fro across the narrow line that separated control from non-control. Of course there were many places where the track crossed stoney ground and after a great deal of pulling and persuasion our pace would drop to an impatient walk. But there were intervening stretches of good soft going not too slimy with the wet, and over these we paced and cantered just within the limit of my muscular endurance. Allowing for the stoney parts, 17 miles in three hours was good quick going and very exhilarating. But when we reached home and I slid from the saddle, every muscle in my arms and back had a separate ache in it, and I felt as one used to feel after hard football games forty years ago. And how those horses ate! I have had to make two corrals because of the fighting at their meals.

*

Bert's ranch is an extraordinarily beautiful place. Park-like gently rolling hills ring it about and give protection from the wind, without in any way shutting the land in. Groves of great noble-looking trees fringe the pretty creek that runs down the little valley's centre. Some seventy acres of first-class soil criss-crossed with irrigation ditches are in alfalfa or are cropped for timothy. There is Bert's house and barn, corrals for cattle, haystacks and outhouses, a wire enclosure for the black and silver grey foxes that Bert's wife breeds very profitably, and across the creek among the cottonwoods my shack and horse corral. But Bert is no rancher — he is of the old days, a horseman above such things, and moreover he earns what he earns far away from home. The boys do not work; their only interest is in driving a car or tinkering with its machinery, both of which things they do very cleverly. So everything about the ranch is down-at-heel. Irrigation ditches are partly effective, partly not; weeds mix in with the crops; farm machinery lies out all year wherever it was last used; tools are left rusting where they were dropped; fences rot and fall over; nothing matters. What the boys are going to do when they are fully grown I cannot conceive. It is hard to picture them earning money. And yet that ranch could carry many sheep (for instance) and be made a soundly paying proposition by reasonable hard work and management. For myself, I would be sorry to see this happen — for Arcadia is so hard to find in these busy commercial days, and being an old-timer in heart myself, I love this place as it is and am in tune with its gentle-minded feckless folk.

* * *

September 26, 1929
Dear Mr. Denny:

In this country where horses are worth anywhere from $5 (or in the case of wild ones, nothing) to $50 (or in the case of extra special ones, $100) and cost of upkeep is shoeing plus a ton of hay for the winter and such oats as an eccentric owner like myself may think of feeding at odd times, it does not feel as stylish to be the owner of four or five horses as it would be in the Old Country. I own four with a vague sort of possessive relation to Dart's mare Dixie, who has been kept for my personal use for several years past. In Arcadia a great many financial and property relations exist in this dim, undefined way, such as the ownership of some of my tools and horse gear. Yesterday I retrieved my wife's pet handsaw from rusting

Letters, 1929

underneath a decrepit Ford car; a hammer from where it had been dropped by the fox pens; and there seem to be still at large since my last visit:

1 horse bit
1 canvas square 7 ft by 7 ft
1 pail
1 box candles
1 axe
1 pick

I know where the axe is — old Dan is using it; and the canvas square may be making a trip to Seattle on board a Ford car. These things may all turn up in time, unless lost. Nothing is ever said — the manner is natural and unconscious, easy-going to the nth degree. *Per contra*, I have to be vigilant to pay my just bills or someone may forget to toll me. And I'm using several articles belonging to other people myself.

*

It is dark now at 4:30 a.m., so at that time, when I dropped off the slowed-down train at Belfort, I had a candle stuck through a hole in the side of an empty tin to light my path down to the shack. I reflected sadly that it was September 25 and that my last visit had ended September 2, chickenpox intervening. There were no horses to greet me, as I had sent no notice of my coming.

When light came I took a nosebag with some oats to help in catching horses, concealed the ropes under my coat and walked up the steep hillside to Bert's 160-acre field, now soundly fenced. On the top flat I spied four horses who soon came up to eye the nosebag. But no Kate — no plump, affectionate little three-year-old on whom this day I had the notion of putting my saddle for the first time. I looked uphill and downhill. Then in the distant grass I noticed something upon which magpies were hopping, and going closer saw it was Kate, dead. She was lying on her side, with no sign of struggle, no bullet mark, no apparent cause of death. Poison was all that I could think of. Friendly little Kate!

Dan McGregor is 82 and his blood pressure is a good deal the worse for early hardship and wild booze jamborees in days not so long since gone by. A tall, silent, deaf, very decent-hearted chap, with grizzled beard that bears evidence of the constant chewing of tobacco, Dan had had Kate for a pet ever since she was foaled. His face fell when I told him that she was dead. We rode up again to see her. Three weeks dead, and poisoned we agreed. And then Dan said, "It makes me sore to think they noticed she was missing and never troubled to look for her and find out why." Which was saying a good deal for Dan. In Arcadia you do not often criticize other people.

That remark of Dan's struck the same thought in me, and soon I was good and mad. I had arranged with Bert for someone to look after my horses; had been guaranteed better service after the fuss about the fallen fence (when my best horse was nearly crippled) and after other episodes — and here Kate had fallen sick and died and I myself, coming from Vancouver, was the first person to know about it. "Rotten," I called it, and thought of blighting things to say to the boys and to Bert. But after a while I cooled off. For these people had not fallen down by their own standards. They have no care for horses, no picture whatever of standards of service and efficiency such as we have had to develop in our business lives. To berate them would be like treating a horse roughly because it acted like a horse. All the same!

So I ended by writing a letter that Bert will get when he next comes home, and in it I asked him to arrange definitely for some reliable *grown-up* person to be responsible for seeing that the horses were looked up once every day, wet or shine, because boys are only boys (even at 18 and 17 as two of his are!) and because I flatly "did not want a horse to sicken and die and no one know about it till I come weeks later and find the body myself." And I told him it was mouldy alfalfa hay sent over to my corral that poisoned Kate. Bert himself will feel these stabs badly, for he has standards regarding a friend's interests. But his boys, who I pay regularly to do the job, and who should have been responsible, will not turn a hair. They will merely be idly surprised that I should waste attention upon such things.

*

Bert's sister-in-law, who, with her husband, lives in a remote little valley among the hills, told me that the deer come browsing round their shack, they are so tame. And there was a bear that used to steal the cottage cheese that she would make and hang up in a white cloth to dry on the wash line. One day when the laundry was all on the line she saw, through the window, a bear on its hind legs walking down the line and flapping a paw at each piece of laundry to see if it held cottage cheese. The bear ended up on the veranda just outside the door and Bert's sister-in-law thought to give it a good scare by opening the door suddenly and saying "Boo." It so happened that the door was locked from the outside so the lady ran to the window. The bear, hearing the rattle of the door knob ran to the window too — and they suddenly looked into each other's faces with only the glass between!

* * *

September 28, 1929
To H.H. Thomas Esq. c/o Thomas Bros. Store, Princeton, B.C.
Dear Bert:

When I was talking to my wife this morning she said, "I feel that you are continually worrying Mr. Thomas about your horses, just as I know you did worry him with all that fuss about Major Taylor and his friends.[19] It isn't the custom anywhere out West to look after horses the way you want them looked after; in any range country horses are supposed to look after themselves almost all the time. It is only near these cities such as out at Lansdowne Park, over at Saanich where Taylor has sent his horses, or at these riding-club stables, or at a place where they breed polo ponies like Hetts on the North

Thompson, that horses are cared for like milking cows are. That is practically what you are after — having them cared for like cows. It is difficult for Mr. Thomas to have that done; and you are all the time worrying him about it. He's too polite to tell you that he and all the family find it a nuisance and an imposition on their good nature."

Well, Bert, my wife has a good head and I thought there was a good deal of sense in what she said, and I want you to be downright frank with me about it as the last thing I would want to do would be to be a nuisance to you all, especially as you are one of my closest friends and I know and like all you folks so well. Having the horses in that field is A-1; the boys getting the horses in for me, taking them back again, and taking them to shoe is A-1 also. The difficulty is in "looking after" them rather, as my wife said, like cows. For instance, when the cold weather comes I don't think those California horses could rustle out on the range the way Nigger or the other local horses do; in fact the thin-skinned little mare may have a tough time anyway (and it might even pay to bring her down here for the cold spell). Hence someone with a grown-up viewpoint looking after them would make all the difference.

Dan might find it too much; my suggestion of Alf is probably quite unsuitable for other reasons: the field is next to Percy's but I don't know whether Mr. Green would do it or whether he savvys the horses the way one wants. There may be someone nearby I haven't thought of. If all this is a fuss and nuisance to you (which I would hate to be the cause of) it might be possible to board the horses at Percy's or Hanson's or Hardwick's (I don't know them) or some other fairly close place and I could have them over to my shack when I come up. Of course that field you have them in is a peach of a place for most of the year — just ideal.

Give it a think Bert, and drop me a line. I sure don't want to bother you and your folks, and yet I'm worried about the matter till we get something thought up.

There's another point that is coming up soon. After thinking things over quietly during my chickenpox attack, I am now really getting at some business and investment changes that will have the two effects of fixing up the wife's finances more on their own, and also of leaving me freer to spend more time up your way. I want at least three and often four days a week up there instead of these miserably short two-day weekends, and I'm going to get it. So easy horse arrangements will mean a lot to me. Tell you more about my plans when we next meet.

* * *

December 11, 1929
Dear Mr. Denny:

A really good piece of news came to us recently, namely that you had resumed nine-mile walking. Walking is such a splendid all-round tonic. I've been reading *Memoirs of a Fox Hunting Man* by Siegfried Sassoon, and while I have never been on a horse in England and don't approve of hunting animals for sport, the book recalls many charming pictures of bygone English countryside life to anyone who (like you and I) has felt the true zest of long hours of country walks. The memoirs are delightfully written, from the very opposite of the hardboiled sporting viewpoint. In memory of the past we knew, and if you have not read it already you might like it, though what one friend likes in books may often be tiresome to another.

*

Friday midnight, on the way up to Arcadia, two loud explosions woke me suddenly, the train stopped dead and an American in the next berth asked the porter if there was a hold-up. However, there were no bandits — it was merely a fragment of the wild scenery of the Coquihalla Pass that had fallen on the line and was being dynamited. But I did not get to sleep again so that, contrary to habit, I turned in for a snooze after reaching the shack at five o'clock. An hour later I thought I heard a shout, but having decided it would be old Dan calling to his dog, I went on snoozing until about seven when two of my horses came tramping in the snow around my bed and snuffling at me. It seemed strange that they had not been fed, for while I am particular to do all my own stable work when at the shack, Dan would be sure to do it if he could catch me napping. So I jumped up and fed them hay and then turned to see young Bill coming with a message.

*

Old Dan must have been a powerful man in his time, tall and big framed. At 82, with high blood pressure, he has to mind his P's and Q's but he will often come over to my place and insist upon using an axe or carrying tree limbs for my fire. Very "high principled" is Dan (as Bert puts it), conscientious and responsible. For instance, he devoted treasures of care to my lame chestnut horse these past three weeks and there have been bottles of liniment and one thing and another in the stable that I know I did not pay for. That is his idea of a job — do it well. And so in the early morning when I see his lantern light moving among the barns across the creek I always boil a fresh pot of coffee and heat some milk and go over for a little chat while Dan sits on the edge of a manger and has a hot drink. With two hours or so of stable work and milking before breakfast is ready at the ranch house, he admits to feeling a trifle faint sometimes.

Bill's message was "Dan's hurt himself; slipped on the ice over near the milkshed." I went over to the house, where Bert and his wife were breakfasting upon porridge, toast and fried potatoes in the kitchen, and in the livingroom, sprawled upon a sofa, was Dan, quiet, uncomplaining, with a hip (so we found afterwards) broken in two places. It was at 6 o'clock that he had fallen and it was his shout that I had heard. No help coming, he had risen to his feet by some astounding effort, only to find that he "could not navigate." Then, getting cold, he had crawled little by little to the ranch house-steps and shouted until Bert woke and heard him.

The doctor in that country looks rather like a slightly qualified veterinary to me, but even at that he may know more about the mountain folk he has to treat than one's educated susceptibilities give him credit for. He went in to see Dan, came out in two minutes, backed his car up against the veranda steps, turned to me and said briskly, "Another of them finished. I can't operate; one chance in fifty for the displaced bones to knit and give him a short stiff leg; otherwise he'll only come out of hospital on a stretcher." Men were sent for, Dan hoisted into the car and off they went on the rough country road. I had a glimpse of Dan, sitting almost erect, face impassive, moustache bristling, black felt hat at a jaunty angle, and never a wince when the car bumped over a rock — dauntless as Clemenceau. There is great stuff in some of those old-timers; time and again there is the austere touch of great tragedy.[20]

*

    I wait for the dawn, these dark winter mornings, dozing before my campfire, comfortable amid the snow. The fire makes a quiet fluttering noise, very peaceful and pleasant, and its smoke coils up among the black shapes of trees which show against the starlit sky. I listen to the distant bark and long-drawn howl of a coyote or to the faint honk from southern flying geese ever so high overhead, and like the great philosopher I think about nothing. When the light comes I begin a day of ceaseless activity. It was Dan's idea to enclose with a wire fence two acres around our shack and to build a little wooden stable with a hayloft over it. So now the four horses have a winter playground and a stable for cold nights, and I am busy with axe and rake and fire, clearing the ground beneath the trees. When darkness comes I bed in a cozy hollow of the ground. Sunday morning there were several inches of snow over my quilt cover. Fourteen degrees of frost is the most so far.
    Pleasure and luxury can come from simple things just as well as from the spending of money. For instance, the luxury of warming cold hands at a campfire; cooking and eating a bowl of porridge when really hungry; resting on a sack in front of the fire or in a dry bedquilt after getting tired and wet. Freedom from the modern tyranny of Time and from Noise and Hustle.

Chapter Five
DOWN SOUTH

What with one thing and another my Summer holidays of 1929 were put off until just before Christmas. Then my wife and I caught a train going South to where Summer weather still might be, and in the early dawn of the next day but one we awoke to see palm trees and orange groves, a skyline of bare hills and the sparkling lights of a little town. Then the sun came up in a clear blue sky and in the pleasant warm air, after months of gloomy Autumn weather in Vancouver, we felt a sudden lightness of spirit like miners coming out from work deep underground, or deep-sea divers released from their suits of lead. No drizzle, snow, chill or wet streets or stuffiness of overheated offices. Also there were no forests to look at. B.C. has too much of their eternal green ...

Even though it was Winter and the volume of traffic light, we shall not easily forget the strange variety upon those desert roads. A high-powered limousine would flick by, at sixty or seventy miles an hour; wealthy people on a tour, making for the next town with good hotels. Then would come businessmen or commercial travellers in their cars, travelling nowadays by road instead of by train; or a big stage with "New York-Los Angeles" upon it. Then campers' cars of every kind, from those of well-to-do people with neat boxes and carry-alls strapped to a good class car, to emigrant families crowded into decrepit Fords that were loaded with huge bundles, mattresses, stoves, flapping canvas, dogs and children. Towards evening campfires gleamed from the roadside where tramps cooked in tins cans or warmed themsleves for sleep, or where tents were pitched alongside family cars. In the outskirts of little settlements those who could afford it spent the night at one of the camping grounds where rows of tiny cabins are for rent, at twenty-five cents, fifty cents, up to a dollar each. We ourselves stayed at hotels, but even so, all day, we belonged to a new world of road folk and saw into the lives of our fellow travellers.

Pleasant it is, and consoling to us who fail to be rich, that happiness exists so cheerfully at every level of poverty or wealth; from the tramp with nothing but a suit of clothes and overcoat, to the tramping family with a Ford car and seventeen dollars plus the hope for work, the retired Ohio farmer and his wife moving to California with their life savings of $1,700 in the bank, and so on up. After all, why not buy a Ford truck, build your house upon it as many do, and call it home? Then you are at home everywhere and life is simple.

Now we know where motor cars go to when they die. Firstly at every sharp bend along these thousands of miles of desert and mountain highways there lie the broken fragments of a car, like the dead shell of some enormous beetle, picked clean of every piece of value. These once belonged to high-speed owners and are a pleasant thing to think of when one of these gentry crowds you almost off the road. But the great sight, unbelievable till seen, is at the camping grounds and garages. Dozens, scores and sometimes hundreds of broken-down, broken-up, half-dismantled cars, car frames, car bodies, car parts, lie around singly and in heaps, relics of the emigrant travel of the past few years. So many single men hunting jobs, or families seeking new homes, contrive to own an almost used-up car. They start for the West hoping to earn something somewhere on the way. Then their money runs out and they can buy no more oil and gasoline, or the car breaks down and they cannot pay for repairs, or the heat of the desert sets the car on fire. They sell it for a song to the nearest garage, or leave it where it stopped — and so these huge car cemeteries are created along the roads.

Chapter Six
LETTERS, 1930

July 30, 1930
Dear Mr. Denny:

As I ride along, twenty-five feet of half-inch rope connects me, as if by telephone, with the horse behind that carries my little pack. Frequent messages pass to and fro along this line: a pull meaning, "We are passing good grass feed;" a sort of dragging, "This bores me, why not stop awhile?"; a jolt as we cross a creek, "Here! I want a drink." Sometimes there is a fullstop at a cross trail that would lead homeward, or at a suitable site for camp. I used to get sore elbows from this jolting on the rope, but now I have a canvas loop around my saddle horse's neck and pass the lead rope through it with a hitch so that the weight of my horse takes the jolt, which discourages idle messages from behind. But my horses like these mountain trips and there is a good deal of reasonableness in what they signal.

The other day a slight unwillingness puzzled me in Dixie. By the time we reached 12-Mile Creek I knew by the rope that there was something wrong and, letting her go ahead of me, soon saw that her left hind leg did not move quite naturally. Then I found a small bent nail dug underneath the frog of Dixie's foot. To work out any poison dirt, I went on slowly to Powder Camp where there is good horse feed, and there by great luck I found Newsy Hill, his tiny tent pitched beneath a tree, bright fire burning and himself in a skimpy bathing suit, cooling off in Whipsaw Creek, for it was very hot weather.

Thirty years ago, in the booming pioneer days, Newsy made money by selling books and papers in Princeton.

Martin Grainger on Dixie, with pack-horses, ca 1928. This photograph was probably taken by Bert Thomas, in the hills west of Princeton. (COURTESY BC ARCHIVES AND RECORDS SERVICE)

Commercial ambition took him to Vancouver, where he lost his money; now he seems to support life by working in a city bookshop part of the year. In his bathing suit, all wet, he stood and poured out talk while I unsaddled, took off Dixie's pack and doctored her injured foot. He told me how man should never live in cities; how he himself had travelled to Australia and Japan on next to nothing, to see the World; how he loved solitude in these mountains, getting up at three o'clock, walking four hours, then observing Nature, bathing, philosophising and catching trout for the rest of each summer day. He seemed to have nothing with him but the bathing suit, trousers, tent, small blanket, two cooking tins, a bag of rice, some nuts, tea, butter and fish hooks. Happy as a lark and about sixty-five years old, as far as I can judge.

Last year, permits were given to settlers to drive two thousand sheep into the mountains for the summer feed that grows so plentifully. There is a transcontinental highway under construction through the Cascades region and much of the mountain region it borders upon will in a year or two be most valuable to the people of the Coast as a natural Park, like Banff (that the Canadian Pacific Railway advertises so much) or like Yellowstone on the American side. I have been urging the Princeton people to take time by the forelock and press the Government to proclaim a Park Reserve; and the sheep this year are being kept north of the suggested boundaries. So it happened, last weekend, that a newspaperman came from Vancouver to make a trip with me over the Summit and back along the route of the future road in order that he could write about this Park project.[21] He was sensible; he submitted to cuticura and talcum powder, strips of puttee tied beneath his knees, seamless leg underwear of mine, a soft sweater to sit upon at first and leather chaps to ease the chafing on his legs and give a better grip upon a horse. I promised not to ride fast downhill, which is difficult and tiring for those not used to it.

That man was good. In the War he had been an artillery driver, but coming straight from a city desk it was a marvel how he stood those strenuous two days. We had two saddle horses each, which we rode turn about, the spare horses carrying a little bedding and our simple food — wholewheat bread, oatmeal, pemmican, pecan nuts, tea and coffee, together with small bags of oats for the horses, since on quick trips like this they must be tied up at night and cannot graze. At 1 a.m. I would arise, kindle the fire, set on the breakfast pots and begin packing up by firelight. The newspaperman would insist on getting up to do his share. He fed the horses, took off the skimpy canvas nightgowns that, in those cool high altitudes, keep the horses warm and fresh for the next day's hard work, and then he would help in packing up and saddling. I myself travel without blankets, with just an aviator's furry suit and a light canvas bag into which I crawl by way of coverlet and tent, and my companion merely had a down quilt with a canvas wrap. So you would think it surprising that the time from our awakening until we would be mounted and leaving camp would be three hours and, in the evening, three hours would pass in looking after the horses and making camp. Nine hours in the saddle and stops during the day to let the horses graze and to eat our own meals, meant that we were on the go for nineteen hours, sleep being practically cut down to little over four.

On our way up, we followed the historic trail that was made by the old fur traders through the Cascade Mountains as far back as 1845 when Oregon and Washington were lost to Great Britain and a new route between Coast and Interior became necessary. At 6,000 feet we struck south along the Summit country; zig-zagged up the Knife Edge Ridge to 7,500 feet and came upon the great moorland shoulders of the Three Brothers peaks, where we camped, with line after line of sawtooth ranges filling the scenery to the far-distant skyline — a sea of mountaintops. Big buck deer would hear our horse bell, stare at us and bounce away. Flowers — scarlet, blue and golden — were everywhere. The sun blazed, the patches of snow we crossed were melting fast, and the beginnings of little creeks tinkled as the water dropped over the rocks.

It is some years since I have gone down the trail from the high country to the Roche River, along which the new highway will pass, and when we came to this part of our journey it took me some time, scrambling on foot on the steep slope, to find the faint markings with which the trail begins. Then for two solid hours we went down, down, mostly in thick timber, peering ahead, missing the trail, refinding it, very thirsty, until at last after five hours in the saddle we reached the Roche and had our midday meal. It was easy going after that, with the horses jogging contentedly along a pleasant trail following the river bank, with beaver cuttings to notice, and squirrels and chipmunks skipping along the trees.

Along towards evening, the sound of horsebells reminded me that the McDiarmid family were camping for the Summer upon a homestead that they had taken up on the route of the new highway. We found them on the river bank, half a dozen youngsters, the widow and a grown-up girl, living in two tents. In a meadow, nearby, their hobbled horses were grazing. The cow (that had lain down so often on the mountain trail when they led it out) was being milked underneath a tree, while tea and jam and junket and campfire bread were set upon a rough-hewn table. So we stopped and camped right there, eating the junket and leaving odds and ends of our own surplus supplies. Sitting round the fire afterwards we talked of the road to be, and of old times, and of horses and wild pets. Mrs. McDiarmid had had a wolverine, a coyote (that could never overcome its shyness), deer, and (most intelligent of all) a tame beaver that, among other games, would make an imitation dam across the kitchen floor with any objects it could find. Rather pleasant it was, with the barefoot children listening as they lay around the fire, the stars overhead and our own fatigue inclining us to drowsiness after the long day's ride.

As I went to bed I felt a little sad to think of the children's father with whom I had camped last year on that very spot. Poor Henry, who, soon after, had fallen from his horse in a faint and taken four hours to crawl a mile to Belge's cabin, where by a miracle some passerby had found him. You will remember my telling you about his death. Henry was a good fellow, fond of the mountain life as the old-timers were.

The citizens of Princeton wished my newspaper friend to see the copper mine upon which their little town so much depends, and the two new coal mines that are being opened, with other goodly matters of advertisement for a community that will be upon a transcontinental highway two years hence. I had promised to deliver him to them, alive or dead, at breakfast time Monday morning. So we arose again at 1 a.m. and flitted silently away from the McDiarmid camp at the first gleam of light. The horses went happily upon the homeward trail. But at Copper Creek, with four mountainous ranges still to cross, it was already six o'clock. I turned my little mare loose to ramble behind us, led the fourth horse, apologized to my newspaper friend and started to make time.

The horses are in fine fettle these days, after so many trips. Their muscles stand out, they climb up like cats, and they will speed along the flat or downhill as fast as I will let them. Until recently, on homeward journeys, it became a free fight every time I dismounted to tighten girths and many an inviting creek I have passed, thirsty, rather than get off and face the fuss and, maybe, have my feet trodden upon or my hands or legs tangled up in reins and ropes while climbing back upon a prancing horse. But now, following an inspiration, I tie the horse I am riding by a slip-knot to a tree; manoeuvre the other horse (or horses, if I should be leading two) into convenient positions; mount with dignity while the saddle horse vainly endeavours to pull down the tree; loose the knot and dash off in comfort. Even so I rarely stop, except to change horses every three hours. Usually I ride one horse, lead another with the pack and have a third loose, following like a dog. But never two horses loose at one time, for one would nudge the other, motion with its head toward the trail and two skylarking animals would soon make up a little party homeward bound upon their own.

With the horses so fit, "making time" meant hard going for any rider not in tough condition, but my newspaper friend never turned a hair. We climbed and climbed; we trotted interminably on twisting trails where the ground was reasonably flat; the horses skipped over fallen trees and among boulders; we went miles down to cross each creek. Up to nine o'clock I kept my promise not to go fast downhill, but then, with the thought of Princeton citizens waiting impatiently in a motor car at the end of highway construction, I let the horses go, and for the last half hour we rattled down the slopes of Kennedy Mountain in a way that must have made my friend behind feel encased in aching muscles and chafing skin. But he came up smiling at the end, with never a murmur and little loss of skin, a most remarkable thing considering how utterly untrained he was.

He went off in the car, leaving his horses tied to a tree among the tents of the road gang's camp, from where someone would fetch them later in the day. I chewed some nuts and started to take my horses home, 17 miles by the bridle path I use in the lower country. It was sizzling hot and windless, 90 degrees in the shade. I had to hang a shirt over my back as the sun blistered me through the singlet in which I ride. But those good horses kept at a steady trot all the way, and about noon I rode up to the ranch house and felt the cool air of the little brook as I watered the horses under the shade of big trees. I was dried to a chip, but tea and a jugful of milk from the tub in the creek soon put that to rights.

Good news met me, for old Dan had broken a boil on Dixie's foot by poulticing and it seemed clear that the nail injury would not lame her, and that she would be able to travel again within a week or two. The other big horse, Coat, who has been lame for over seven months, was also plainly better, though I am not yet sure that the spavin (which he is now pronounced to have) will ever permit him to go on these hundred-mile weekend endurance trips which I enjoy so much.

I watched the two horses I had been riding exchange salutations with Coat and Dixie — much whinnying, nickering, snuffing of noses together; dismounted stiffly; tumbled my equipment in disorder on to the floor of our shack; cleaned myself a little; drank the tea and milk aforesaid; and went across to the ranch house for boy Bill to drive me the five miles into town to catch the train. There is only one train a day.

In the blistering sunlight, Bill dripped with sweat as he bent over two inner tubes on the ground. It was as if some form of spotted disease covered those tubes; little patches were all over them. Bill had a flat tire, with his ramshackle car jacked up and one wheel off. It was train time and I thought ruefully of my business engagements of the morrow.

Bill would pump on a tire, run to the creek and hold it under water to see where the leaks were; rush back and stick on patches; then abandon that tire and try the other. His outer tires are worn so that in places you can see the inner tubes. Punctures mean little to him, or disarranged carburetors, or fan belts that do not work, or strange noises in the machinery. Somehow in spite of these his car contrives to go. But as Bill worked feverishly at those tires I heard the train whistling at the hill crossing where we should have met it, and I left Bill and sat out on the road hoping that a car would pass on its way to town and planning what to do after I had missed the train. But no car came, nor noise of starting motor from where Bill worked. The distant rumble of the train ceased and I had given up all hope when suddenly Bill's engine started and the car tore out. I jumped in; Bill "hit her up" to thirty-five; we bumped over the ruts and stones of the country road; I dissuaded Bill from fifty, telling him that I was too old for that; and, marvellous to say, we beat the train to Princeton.

The newspaperman and I shook hands with the assembled citizens, boarded the Pullman car (looking like ruffians), stretched out on the seats and lost consciousness. We woke up once, on the journey home, to drink milk and eat fruit in the little old dining car of this branch line of the C.P.R., then slept again until the night porter shook our shoulders and woke us at Vancouver. I taxied home, through the brilliant streets, ablaze with neon signs, recounted the events of the trip to my lady, removed dust and grime in a much needed hot bath and fell into bed. Next morning sitting in my office chair, all this seemed mere memory of a dream. Except that somehow I did not want to make the least bodily movement.

* * *

October 14, 1930
Dear Mr. Denny:

You or the ladies are partly to blame for these dreadful gaps in my letter-writing, for the fine suggestion you people made that I ought to write occasional articles for magazines about my mountain Arcadia must have gone a little to my head. No articles resulted, for I know myself too well, but four or five long scribblings have accumulated in my writing case — unfinished for the simple reason that I wanted to rewrite them better, practising the art of literature upon you as it were.

*

I rode into Princeton at 8 a.m. and tied my two horses to a telephone pole in the main street just outside the smithy. There is a battered old hotel across the road with blistered wood pillars and a veranda, where old-timers sit in the sun and watch anything that passes. One of them called to me, "Hi, the smith's sick!" but the man himself came along just then and all he had the matter with him was a stiff neck where the steel of the railway line had caught him when his car upset the day before. The car was going fast and turned over twice, and one of the smith's boys had his legs broken, but a Scottish smith built like a gorilla cannot be killed that way.

While he shod my horses, with a bottle of beer to each two shoes for the ease of his neck, the smith told me that young Penney had come into town on a new horse the previous Wednesday and when opposite the hotel the horse reared and fell over backward, so that Penney was in hospital. Then I walked down the street to buy some eggs (which subsequently broke inside my shirt when Dixie became fussy on the way home), and met old Podunk Davis walking to the beer parlour and using a cane.²²

Podunk had been riding his big grey horse to town. Along the road, at high speed, came a wedge-shaped cloud of dust and machinery which was young Burr on a motorcycle. The grey horse had the bright idea of swerving at right angles across the roadway, then it reared. With a little more clearance

Willard Albert *"Podunk"* Davis. (COURTESY BC ARCHIVES AND RECORDS SERVICE)

Burr and the motorcyle would have passed underneath, but as it was, Podunk, grey horse, Burr and the motorcycle plunged into the roadside brush in a heap together. Podunk's nose was ground into gravel by the horse's weight so that it swelled magnificently, and Podunk's knee was considerably twisted. Young Burr and the motorcycle went to hospital and the grey horse, after regaining its wind, was unaffected.

The point about the story is this: Podunk, who is only seventy-seven, has two old men out at his ranch — ranch meaning a log cabin plus a few fences that tend to keep stray animals out of a patch of hay that the old men cut for winter horsefeed. One of the old men (who didn't oughter because he is subject to sinking spells) went hunting for a stray horse and did not return. Word was sent to Podunk, who was recuperating in Town with the aid of the beer parlour after his accident. He saddled the grey horse forthwith and rode all day, twisted knee and all, hunting for the missing man whose footmarks were hard to follow in that wooded country, even for Podunk who is good at that sort of thing. There was no tragedy — the old man, after a sinking spell, had spent the night under a tree and then, in five hours, had walked three miles to a trail where he was found. But Podunk when telling me about this was wondering why his knee should be a "bit sore".

I had a mind to chop away some saplings that had fallen across the bridle path that leads from Princeton to the high mountains, so that day after the shoeing I, with axe tied to the saddle, started out, leading the little mare Bessie. She seemed disinclined to come and dragged on the lead rope, a very annoying habit with some horses but not a habit of hers. The dragging became worse and worse until, rather angrily, I changed horses. To my astonishment, after riding a few yards, Bessie went off the trail, right into a tree. I pulled her round and a moment or two afterwards she slipped off the edge of a gravel bank so that I nearly came out of the saddle. Something was plainly wrong. The little mare had gone stone blind!

Old Dan was very kind. Three times a day, for weeks, he put into Bessie's eyes the various drops that the veterinary sent. He kept her by day in a dark stable and let her wander in my corral at night, with a horse kept in to give her company. It worried him that she should whinny as she did, standing with her head up and ears pricked forward, listening for answering whinnies from the hills; a thing of beauty, with her neck arched like an Arab, her neat firm muscles, cream colour, flowing white mane and tail. There was some abscess in the sinus above her eyes and in the end Bert had to shoot her. Now he may have to shoot my big hunter, for after ten months he still goes lame. So the vicissitudes multiply! One of the mountain coal mines near the little town had an explosion about that time and forty-eight men were killed.

On the less serious side of life, we have had unloaded on us by letter of introduction a typical old-style remittance man, unfortunately without the remittances. He made a creditable start but there was a little something in the eyes (what *is* it that tells one?) which held our judgment in suspense and now the old familiar symptoms are coming out, in profusion. Booze and the borrowing of money — even from confiding taxi drivers! There is a question now of his working a passage home — but how can one recommend him to a captain? Work for him here is out of the question, there are 10,000 unemployed for city relief as it is.

Which reminds me that the hold-up season has started early this year. The daily papers are helped out greatly by the number of burglaries, sluggings and daylight robberies at revolver point. Near Flavelle's mill a stage driver was held up by four men who thought the Imperial Oil Company's payroll was in his bus, but he grabbed one of their revolvers and put them to flight, wounding one.[23]

It is queer how people's minds get used to the idea that this sort of thing is going on in the city in which they live. It seems far away and of very little interest to them until they get caught themselves. We are tinged with the American indifference to crime. In Canada most of the hold-up men are mere hungry amateurs and usually mean no harm, though the man from the Burglar Alarm Company showed my wife a bullet scar on his hand and told her there was a bad bunch now in town, and that the police advice was to put up your hands at once when requested to do so and to give the man with a gun whatever he wanted, because he might be a "dope" (addict) and irresponsible. Did you know that the narrow silver line often seen as an ornamental border on jewellers' windows is in reality tinfoil with an electric current running through it from a central station at a Burglar Alarm Company's office? If the window is broken the current stops, a bell rings at the station where two men with automatics jump into an armoured car and speed to the broken window.

What a change, this year, in people's minds. Gone is that hectic interest in the stock market and lavish living. Did you get the "new thrift" in England? It is an invention of U.S. economists and industrial leaders — the duty of spending all you had as fast as you could and so increase prosperity. But now last year's car is plenty good enough, the divorce rate has fallen along with stocks, and ladies do their own housework again. The slump, of course, has had a poisonous effect upon one's most conservative investments, but even so we feel that it is a much nicer world to live in than it was a year ago. But poor people out of jobs must be having a tough time, with no relief in sight. Some of us, disillusioned elders, incline to the idea that what we have gone through so far in 1930 may be a mere curtain raiser to the deeper depression of this Winter because all this wage cutting, discharging and loss of profits in trade must surely have a cumulative effect. But the professional economists are modestly hopeful, though their forecasts are apt to be tinged by propaganda. All the Hearst newspapers had orders, months ago, to be "prosperity papers", i.e to feature good news and put bad news on the back page, in small type.

Chapter Seven
TRAVELLING LIGHT

I had come over the mountains to the trails west of the Cascades and, being pressed for time, was travelling late when my saddle horse, who had been picking his way in the pitch darkness goodness knows how, sprang sideways and gave a snort. In the silence of night this sort of thing gives a person the creeps, but as I thumped him forward with my heels the embers of a tiny fire came into sight and a figure reared up suddenly from a bed alongside the trail.

It was the famous Miss Allen, the hospital nurse of sixty-two, who every Summer goes on a mountain walking tour. She it was who was lost, some years ago, in the Summit country, twenty-five days without other food than a few berries, snow on the ground, a thin shawl around her shoulders and the tatters of a dress left after she had used most of it to bind to her feet the fragments of a pair of shoes. The old prospector who found her has never ceased to marvel at such endurance, greater than he has known among lost people in all his thirty-five years of wandering in these mountains. But women are like that — they stand exposure better than men and get less crazed in mind — though I've heard that prospector say that Miss Allen must have been out of her head at times during those twenty-five days, for in trailing her he found a place where she had "wallowed around a log like a bear," round and round, leaving bloodstains where the brush had cut her legs. Anyway, she was no worse for it, though her hair fell out afterwards and then grew again.[24]

The horses ceased to fuss when they heard Miss Allen's voice, and I sat in the saddle chatting with her and answering questions about trails, about some of which she knew very little. Then I passed on into the night and so back to business in the city.

It was raining, a week later, when I passed again the brush bed and sloping stick above some ashes that showed where Miss Allen had camped that night. By afternoon, when I reached an old abandoned ranch house near the international boundary, the rain was pelting down and 5,000 feet above, where the old trail climbs the shoulder of Hozameen, there were whirling clouds with dismal black ridges dimly seen. It looked most unpleasant, but what was a person to do? Very dull to backtrack forty miles to Hope in the Fraser Valley, worse to lay up for better weather while people became apprehensive at one's non-arrival home, and with only fifteen pounds of oats for two hungry horses. So after a hot meal cooked in the old house that a romantic Englishman built and deserted twenty-five years ago, I started up the overgrown trail on which showed clearly the marks of a woman's shoes.

Rip went my silk slicker, from head to foot, on the first bush we pushed through. After that it was just wet. Trees and brush loosed showers of water; the horses slipped and scrambled in greasy clay; the rain poured; and when we emerged from timber onto the open mountain shoulder the wind blew great guns. Here and there, in sheltered places, Miss Allen's tracks were still visible and I wondered if I should find her camped somewhere above. The horses' ears were flat back; they balked at times; the saddle horse kicked at my foot whenever I touched him with a spur. Vain as I may be (in an elderly meek way) to be a tough guy, I surely had my fill of it. But then again, what else to do but keep going? That nurse was sticking out the storm, anyway, with the merest pretence of a blanket, a silk tent, a few pounds of food and not even a hand-axe for making fires. Here was I with two strong horses and a kit perfect for all weathers, with the exception of that absurd torn raincoat.

It was too early in the year to be really cold. When at last we were over the ridge and on the slippery descent to a fold of the mountain where there is camping ground, I even got quite warm on foot, leading the two horses. But there were no signs of Miss Allen's campfire. I tied the horses underneath a tree,

Mary Warburton, Grainger's "Miss Allen". (COURTESY BC ARCHIVES AND RECORDS SERVICE)

cooked supper by the light of a miraculously made fire and so to bed, too tired and washed out to put up any shelter — rain pouring, wind blowing, everything wet except the horse blankets just underneath the saddles, where it matters. This was the great storm that washed out the main line of the Canadian Pacific Railway.

At four a.m. next morning there was thick fog and lying in a pool of water inside my sleeping bag, I wondered what to do. There was fine horse feed all around and a person could doubtless make a fire and put up a canvas shelter and be comfortable though damp until better weather came. The horses were looking daggers at me, with ears tight back, as the drips of the tree pattered heavily upon them, but in their canvas nightgowns they would be right enough. The difficulty about staying in that place was the need for getting home more or less on time and, besides, suppose the rains should turn to snow?

So I emerged from the semi-warmth of the sleeping bag and used all the arts to get a fire going and gave the horses

Travelling Light

very little oats and grazed them some and had a warm breakfast and saddle-up (all of which took ages to do). Around about nine o'clock I rode off into the fog. Soaked as it was, the loose mountain soil kept giving under the horses' feet. As they scrambled they would grab hungrily at the good feed alongside the trail. While I pulled up one horse's head the other would get his down so that for hundreds of yards at a time we would go slowly, almost foot by foot. In grassy places where the ridges flatten out the trail would disappear. Then I would prowl around in the rain and fog to find some stunted alpine tree to which to tie the horses while I circled and slid on the wet grass to find the trail again. This must have happened twenty times during the day, partly because of my dim and very wrong memories of the way that trail should go.

Even with all this walking the incessant soaking made my teeth chatter. When at last we slid and scrambled down the long sidehill descent to the first lake east of the Cascades and I dipped water for my supper, it was as if someone had boiled the lake, the water felt so warm. But there were no signs of Miss Allen; indeed, for some hours back it had seemed to me that she had not come that way. She must therefore have continued on along the Summit ridges at 6,500 or 7,000 feet elevation, in the heart of the storm. I pushed on to a sheltered place in the valley, made a roaring fire, fed the last of the oats to two loudly-whinnying horses, and filled myself up on rolled oats and pemmican cooked together as a meat pudding, while listening to the wind and pelting rain and thinking of that elderly woman lying in the wet, without a fire, somewhere high above.

The rain had dwindled to a drizzle and almost ceased when I came down to Cambie Crossing. At the ricketty little bridge the bars were up, which made me think that someone with horses might be around. There is a forest ranger's cabin nearby and as I went to it there was a wisp of smoke hanging in the damp air. Miss Allen came out of the cabin, trim in her riding breeches and outdoor shirt. Yes, she said, she had been caught in the storm and been very wet in spite of the silk tent wrapped around her shoulders. Now she was drying out at the cabin and being very scrupulous about using the ranger's cut firewood. She made me a cup of beef tea and offered hospitably some wholewheat wafers out of her small supply.

I sat on a block of wood, warming my sodden clothing at her insufficient fire and she plied me with questions about the trail over Three Brothers, of which she knew nothing, but proposed to take. After all, I supposed, she could hardly get lost on those open summits if she kept to the height of land and picked up the trail here and there. What seemed tough to me was that she carried no handaxe, depending upon dry twigs from underneath trees to start her fires. At the beginning of her trip her pack had weighed but twenty-five pounds — silk tent, bedding and food for three weeks — and though she said she was a very light eater, there must have been little bedding. Nor would she take spare food of mine, except a handful of almonds. After working hard for her living ten months in the year, she felt the need of freedom from things that load one down. Travelling light was her hobby, as it should be.

I have often heard city people say that a woman who liked to wander by herself among the mountains must be a bit queer in the head. But why? You will find friends willing to rough it with you in order to catch more fish than they can eat, or to shoot at any wild animal they see; and others who will pay high Nature a brief visit with a guide, packer and cook — airbeds, tents, canned foods and a pack train to carry it all. But if you travel light you are obliged to go alone. That nurse was no more queer in the head than I am, if that be sanity. She talked to me about her pleasure in the mountain scenery, so fine to look at after being shut away for months among sick people and city buildings; in pure free air after the stuffiness of rooms; in watching the graceful running of the deer or, once in a great while, the sight of a bear; in sitting at a campfire after the day's fatigue and being so conscious of the stars at night. It all seemed sensible enough to me, if a person likes that sort of thing.

I told her, as a matter of professional curiosity, she being a nurse, that in my own case, after arthritis and nervous indigestion and other effects of the high pressure business life, here I was, at 57, soused to the skin for days with never a twinge of rheumatism — great testimony to the healthiness of trail life.

Travelling Light

Before I left Cambie Crossing I gained one last impression of the lady's tranquil mind. I had taken down the bars at the bridge entrance and gone perhaps ten yards over the loosely laid decrepit puncheons, leading my horses, when there was a double crash behind me — both horses down. With a great clatter of hoofs they rose and fell again, and this time the packhorse in his struggle smashed some four feet of puncheons, fell half through the bridge and stuck there with his forelegs doubled under him. Somehow I got the saddle horse across the rest of the way and then, while cooking pots and oddments fell into the stream below and drifted away, I spent most of an hour getting the pack off the second horse. His rear end sat upon a beam beneath the bridge, with a hind leg flailing air on each side, but he is a young horse and supple and, surprisingly, he kept his head, otherwise it would have been a case of chopping down the bridge.

When it was all over, and nobody hurt, and I had fixed both bridge ends so that no other unsuspecting traveller could cross the rotten structure, I went back to tell Miss Allen. Yes, she had heard the crash, she said, and thought it must be a bear! She remembered a noise like that one night the year before when she was caught by snow in crossing Hozameen range from the east, late in the Fall. I had not heard of this adventure before but it seems that she was overtaken by a storm, lost the dim trail (which she had never travelled before), was at times waist-deep in snow drifts, but finally, in the course of days, worked her way down the slopes, through timber and everything, until she reached an old ranch house in the Skagit valley. How's that, I ask you, for a woman of sixty-two?

Chapter Eight
LETTERS, 1931

February 25, 1931
My Dear Norman:[25]

It was nice of Aunt Nellie to send me a copy of your books of verses and I have just been writing to tell her how much I enjoyed reading them. I envy your intensity of impression and Greek ability to extract Life's full value as it passes. To one who sojourns in American cities among folk drugged with the toxins of business thinking and stale air, the glorious Present is very dim. Who, in an office, knows whether the sun shines or not, or birds sing?

Personally, after twenty years, I am gradually escaping from the barbarian temple through a love of exercise and (consequently) of horses. Long weekend trips with two of them (sometimes it has been three) on the high mountains, doing everything for oneself, long hours daily in the saddle and long others in making and breaking camp, pasturing the horses, cooking simple meals at campfires under the stars — this gathers a few rosebuds while ye may and drives away dull Work, the American God.

Ruminating on your verses, it is amusing how the same feeling in two people shows itself in different ways. Could I match your felicity of expression I would write of the ascetic urge, the ceaseless effort to reduce food and covering to their bare essentials (so as to travel light), the perception of elegant simplicities, as in going to bed on hard ground underneath a tree by the mere act of taking off one's boots. I get fussed by all the paraphernalia of living, but people like you, in England, know how to make it beautiful.

* * *

April 16, 1931
Dear Mr. Denny:

After five months absence I am back again at weekends in Arcadia. Once again time ceases to exist except for the coming of light or darkness. I live in the weather, comfortable before a campfire even in a high wind, doing everything for myself except shoeing the horses. That means a lot of physical exertion and the overcoming of many discomforts. One thing that is the matter with many men nowadays is that they have too many things done for them.

I had hung everything in canvas sacks from the ceiling of my shack so as to avoid damage from rats and mice, and all this material had to come down and be sorted and re-packed; saddlery had to be oiled and soaped; and there was a great deal of mending and patching to prepare for the coming season. I made an excellent cotton sweater out of two towels, a far better article than can be bought in any shop, also a pair of overalls that will not drag at the knee nor chafe one in the saddle, and many other similar things. What with chopping wood, cleaning up the shack and horse corrals and exercising the horses, I have every muscle tired each week when I get on board the train for home.

I took the horses into Princeton to get them shod and found the little town very flat financially. At the big copper mine nearby, miners had lived high during the boom years, up to the hilt in instalment buying, and now they are all broke and have to be put on road relief work, much to the indignation of the ranchers and other old-timers who are also broke but who have never enjoyed high wages. The American standard of living is in for a good deal of de-bunking just now, thank goodness. I met old Belge (who I think is seventy-seven) learning to drive a dilapidated fourth-hand car, and Podunk Davis has come into real money, some distant relative having left him $3,000, so he is rich for life.

On my way back home, when the mare had been a little bumptious, I was struggling with the remains of a dozen eggs that were shattered over my clothes and saddle, when a spry young man (as he seemed) came trotting down the trail. It was old Dan, fit as a fiddle, he of the broken hip bone, the high blood pressure and the local doctor's diagnosis of dropsy. Old Dan at 80-odd is cutting two new teeth and he feels good. I had a nice talk with old Burr who runs an auto garage. He was indignant at the slaughter of deer along the new highway construction last Winter. Sportsmen came in dozens and killed from their motor cars. The deer up there have always been on friendly terms with the few prospectors and riders like myself who come into that country. Finally I had long talks with my friend Bert, who comes and sits before my campfire and asks me where the deuce the city folks get with all their fussing about money. Bert is a gentleman — he has time to think.

The horses showed precious little interest in me when I first met them, but they fell immediately into their old habits. The buckskin horse pounds on my veranda steps at 2:30 a.m., the mare kicks an empty feed box along the ground with a loud clatter, and, if these noises fail, one of them will come and drag at my canvas blanket cover where I lie beneath a tree. Canvas, you understand, is linked with the thought of oats which are fed in canvas nosebags. In fact, these horses cadged from me so much that the buckskin developed a touch of gout — he became tender-footed, Bert said, from cracked heels due to the heating of his blood from too much oats — that is as it may be. But it is rather pleasant to have a horse nuzzling over your shoulder when you are eating porridge, and making little noises at you. We live together so much that our understanding of each other is very close. I have made a padded bridle that will make it very comfortable for any horse to be led on trips — there will be no harsh lumps of halter to wrench its jaw.

Arcadia has had a mild Winter and when you ride up the range you see the horses and cattle are fat underneath the fuzzy coats of Winter hair that they are just shedding. Everywhere there are newly-born foals and calves, parties of horses grazing or lying flat in the sun, larks and woodpeckers, nice new grass and flowers beginning to show, and I am now ready for hard trips with a hundred little improvements in trail equipment.

*

Letters, 1931

During the week the city has been giving us some new emotions. We were burgled some years ago and there is only some imitation jewellery in our apartment for thieves to take — they do not bother with silver things — but last Autumn so many hoodlums drifted down to spend a warm Winter in Vancouver along with the thousands of unemployed, that hold-ups and burglaries have become commonplace. So we had electric burglar alarms put on our windows near the fire escape. Once or twice the alarm has gone off when we have been moving windows ourselves — a horrid raucous sound on a big gong — and recently the janitor heard the alarm going when no one was at home and thought that the high wind might have shaken the window down until the electric contact was made. There is some doubt about this.

Anyhow, when I was awakened from deep sleep at 12:30 a night or two ago, I stupidly dashed for the gong to see what was the matter, and lost a few precious seconds before meeting my wife and running to the window. One's wits are not at their brightest on a sudden awakening of that kind, and after various excursions in which my wife saw a man hurrying away, we both went to bed. Next morning in the street-car a neighbour told me that he had four locks crowbarred off his garage door in the past 12 nights. It is quite useless to inform the police, who are lost in all this welter of hold-up and petty theft.

*

As for the Depression, goodness knows when we are to get rid of this massive unemployment. Every day we hear of further discharges of employees. I was interested at Princeton railway station to see the the local constable forcing a number of men to mount the coal tender of the locomotive of our train and go somewhere else. There are now two streams of men travelling free on freight trains and engines in search of work, one stream going East, one West. Conditions on the Prairies are bad, just as they are here, but bank directors in the East and statisticians declare that the turn is taking place, though its symptoms are very modest yet. The trouble is that bankers and statisticians have lied so steadily for 18 months that who can now believe them? There is an interesting article in this month's *Scribner's* about the cyclone effect of this Depression upon the white-collar classes in the United States. It mentions how the Young Women's Christian Associations have been crowded with wives of all ages learning again to be stenographers and filing clerks to help out husbands who have lost their jobs. It mentions that one large bank merger in 1930 threw 10,000 employees out of work. Some of the discharging has been hard-boiled; men of many years' experience have had a fortnight's or a month's curt notice. A very different attitude towards the high-pressure American business system is being developed among men who have been treated thus, and everywhere you hear talk of what is being done in Russia. The change from the talk of 1929 and the deification of Henry Ford and Hoover is astounding, but in Arcadia, where there are tubs of rich milk cooling in the creek and eggs and surreptitious deer meat, the Depression merely means less money, gasoline and cars to carry people up and down the roads unncessarily.

* * *

May 5, 1931
Dear Mr. Denny:

Among others hard hit by the Depression are polo players, many of whom cannot afford to play this season and must dispose of their horses. So it came that I rode into Princeton at half past five on Saturday morning to meet a freight train upon which was a polo pony whose owner wished me to take care of it for a year. As the freight drew up at the station I noticed a car in which a farmer, his wife and children, some cows, chickens in coops, and the family furniture were all on their way to somewhere else. When I scrambled up through the half-open door of the car I found, nestling in the straw, 14 sleeping men. One of them was curled up almost between the legs of the little horse. Playing-cards were scattered upon the floor and there was an empty flagon of loganberry wine.

Altogether there were 29 men on that freight, some clean, some dirty, some old, most of them young. They stood round uncomfortably in a drizzling rain while shunting was being done, then jumped aboard again as the train moved east. How all this moving army of unemployed manages to eat puzzles me. Policemen (they call them "the bulls") come down at every train stop and oblige men without money to keep on travelling. I cannot conceive that shops and housekeepers along the line can afford to give out food. It is said among railway men that the day in March when Vancouver cut off relief to single men, 700 jumped one single train going East. And, sadly enough, there is a parallel stream seeking work westward. They tell me that as one car of an arriving freight stopped at Vancouver the door opened and 65 men were counted as they hopped out and went uptown.

I give these figures for what they are worth. They are doubtless somewhat exaggerated, but the picture is there and mainline travel must evidently be in big volume compared to what I see on a quiet branch line. The old porter on my weekend train told me 38 porters had been laid off at Vancouver by the C.P.R., among the recent discharge of 560 men in B.C. I talked to a hotel man I know who was on the train and he told me that the C.P.R. hotel at Vancouver had been losing $750 a day since the first of the year. Great material in all this for the "biggest boom the country has ever had" predicted by the head of the American Telegraph & Telephone Company a week or two ago, or *Babson's* forecast of business activity that will create a labour shortage in the coming Autumn!

The station agent did not offer to help me unload the horse, and I was ruefully regarding the station crowbar which (with my tender feet) I was unable to use for breaking down the wooden bars nailed across the car door, when a big burly man came hurrying down the little town and asked me anxiously if the freight had gone. As it had, he helped me and when I said, "Let's go and get breakfast" his face lighted up. Over an enormous steak he told me of his winter spent on the

American side in Spokane. In that city an old brewery had been fitted up as rough barracks for destitute men. But he had eked out by getting two or three temporary jobs (which he lost as soon as the employers realized that he was not an American citizen), and he had a room in a house owned by an old lady who let lodgings. All Winter, he said, that old lady gave free board to eight shop girls and stenographers who were flat broke, just to keep them off the streets.

He had spent much time in the warmth of the public library and he'd read a lot, books and even Old Country papers, and talked with other men about what he read — causes of the Depression, the World situation and what not. Being a Scot of five generations settled in Cape Breton, he appreciated the way Old Country papers gave the plain facts and faced them. The American papers were all for hiding things up in a smoke-screen of forced optimism. In a hard-headed way he was against Communism, but eight months of bumming around and encounters with policemen ordering him to move on from every town where he sought work had made him fiercely discontent with the economic mess. As for the unemployed, he said, there would be violent doings if things continued as bad until next Winter. Men's characters were deteriorating by loafing and distress, and the Americans seemed to have no plan whatever for meeting unemployment. I left him at the bench in the blacksmith's shop where the horse was being shod and all the old-timers out of jobs who sit there from morn till night agreed with his views.

*

Buck Allison had been breaking some horses for old Tom Kenyon over on Five-Mile and there was a big brown horse so gentle you could put your arms round its neck right at the start that he said I ought to see. My horses have to be gentle for various reasons. One, I should confess, is that I would at once fall off the other kind. And besides, the horses and I live together in a sort of family way and snorty ones with tough ways are not welcome. The big mare is not all she might be in this way, for she spent part of the weekend running up and down the fence of the corral in which I had, for safety, put the new horse. Her ears were back and her bared teeth snapped at him; she swung and humped her quarters and every little while I heard the clatter of her hoofs on the corral fence. However, she will get used to him after a while, and already the buckskin horse has stopped kicking at him too, and come down to almost playful biting. The little polo pony is quite debonair about such goings on. And you ought to have seen his stare at the country scenery (in which he was brought up) as the car door opened, and heard him snort! City stables are just horse jails.

*

Old Dan went into Town last week, all dolled up in a new suit of city clothes, and he took a room at the best hotel. The great man, his cousin, arrived and they met — after 50 years. They would sit at the hotel window and talk about their clan, then move up to the river bridge and sit there and talk. And old Dan, with rake and axe and shovel and fire, had cleaned up the usual disorder round the ranch buildings so that his cousin could find it nice, and his shack was in a tidy condition I have never seen before. Altogether the cousin's visit was a tremendous event. Old Dan rarely talks of his past, but something about the polo pony reminded him of the time, 40 years ago, when he took a contract for mail delivery in the back regions of Montana where there were no roads and he had to ride 86 miles a day, never in more than eleven hours and sometimes in eight. Ten horses he had, in relay, and the little ones like the polo pony had served him best.

These old-timers have been tough. I rode over the hills and had supper with old Tom Kenyon, with casual reference to the brown horse that Buck Allison had spoken of. It was with Tom that the famous train-robbing outlaw Bill Miner lived for two years in time gone by, and Tom is reputed to have held the horses on the last hold-up on the C.P.R. But one does not refer to that, of course. The last time I saw old Tom he was sitting on the edge of his bed with several ribs stamped in by a wild horse, and other damages. But here he was tilling his fields on a Sunday (having by mistake kept Sunday on the day before) with three mules and a disgusted horse harnessed together, as active as you please. It was late before his excellent meal was cooked and we sat talking till nearly one o'clock in the morning and no moon showing. So I accepted his bed and he crawled in with his hired man. (Etiquette is you take off your coat and trousers and socks.) But I could not forget that the big mare was tied out at the corral fence and the night was not warm, so I arose silently at 3:30 when light began to come and saddled her and went my way.

It was a scene of marvellous beauty as I rode home over the hills — dawn and its colours, the new clean greens of the grass and weeds, the whiteness of snow-capped mountains, and the parties of horses lying asleep or grazing in utter content, with lots of good feed and no flies to bother them. I came across my big chestnut, who since he went lame has found himself a job bossing a bunch of horses and foals. He and the mare, who used to be devoted, seemed to take no notice whatever of each other. But you never can tell — horses exchange many slight attitudes of eyes and head and ears that we humans fail to detect. So I came home to breakfast and before train time exercised the new horse, who springs to a start and is "rearing to go," the buckskin who had taken to stumbling and is like a lump of lead this year, and the big mare, who at 16 years old and very fat, thinks she is a race-horse and would like to run away. Old Dan promised to take her to the pasture by herself for fear the new horse might be kicked on the way there. Then they ran me up to the train and I slept all the way to Vancouver.

* * *

May 26, 1931
Dear Mr. Denny:

Two years ago my wife came camping in Arcadia at (as it happened to my discredit) the height of the mosquito season.

Martin Grainger waiting for the train. (COURTESY RUPERT SCHEIDER)

So this time she and her sister, her niece Constance and 2 1/2-year-old grandnephew Rollo, came early in May when the hills blaze with wild sunflowers and the mosquitoes have not yet been hatched out.

There was a great cleaning of the shack. My belongings (ropes, horse blankets, saddles, packbags and what not) poured out of the porch door in a sort of heavy foam — sheets and blankets and clean things from town went in instead. Not that my clothes were dirty. Had I not, in a panic, the week before taken two years' washing to the ranch house across the creek and borrowed the use of Mrs. Thomas' new motor washing-machine for 17 minutes by the clock? Even the horse blankets went through in that frenzy.

Womenfolk dote on water, so we made a little flume that delivered water from the corral pump to the open-air fireplace. There was also a building of meat safes because the ladies dislike flies. Ropes were stretched between trees so that horses would not come and stamp on the doorstep for oats or swipe the breadstuffs. My sister-in-law slept in the stable which the horses never use, for they feel as I do that four walls, a roof and a door are all hard things to endure and true home is out in the weather. There was a tent too, and it was arranged that the horses would not blare to each other at night and wake people up. I rigged my usual camp out in the corral just as if on a journey.

Cream was one great difficulty. The milk was full of it, thick clotted cream. Old Dan kept appearing at all hours with cans and cans. "Only be thrown away otherwise," he said. They made cream cheeses and sent them to friends, so that my pockets and saddlebags, jogging into town, became soggy with leakage from parcels; they made mayonnaise sauce and ate cream to the danger point; suffered in feminine hatred of waste; and told Dan not to bring so much and he only brought more, being a bit hard of hearing. His last act, as the car came to take us away for the train, was to bring four great jars of cream.

It is astonishing how busy a group of such people can keep themselves, camping. What with nine miles of morning ride to fetch supplies from town, to which Constance and myself elected ourselves for the sake of exercise (and believe me a person and horse hung with parcels like a Christmas tree can give the person lots of perspiration), and meals and getting firewood and looking after four horses and warning Rollo not to go near horses' heels, and looking after Rollo from early morn till dark, our four people worked hard. Besides this the ranch folks took the visitors for motor drives (when the car was not broken down) and we rode over the range to various places — to a roundup where there was a brown horse to look at; over to old Tom Kenyon's where there was another horse, a magnificent creature, a lulu, the mystery of whose secluded past I am trying to divine from cryptic remarks by Tom and others. And at one place boys had dug out a coyote den and all my folks drove over to see the downy little cubs. And then, of course, horse vicissitudes always crowd out leisure time. One day, after lunch, I was sitting by the creek, holding a long tether rope so that the borrowed polo pony (who is scared of ropes) could have a nice graze at the edge of the crops. The day was perfect — blue sky, air scented with pine needles and Balm of Gilead, wildflowers, water tinkling, and hummingbirds.

Letters, 1931

Life was giving perfect happiness. Yet within the hour the big mare, cavorting round the corral, kicked Rollo head over heels. Everyone rushed, there was a smother of bloody towels and iodine, a car to the doctor in town, three people to hold the struggling Rollo while the doctor worked; then the relief of finding that the iron shoe had glanced from the little boy's skull without breaking it. Another time the polo pony, tied by the haystacks, caught a foreleg in his rope and fell against barbed wire — so there was a six-inch gash to bind up and protect from flies, and one horse laid up. Once the buckskin, Ribbons, tangled a hind leg in a grazing tether rope and busted his bridle in three places, a repair job for me. Again, while my wife was visiting a lark's nest by a fence, he caught his bit in the wire and there was another smash to mend. And so on — many reasons why, from 4:30 a.m. till dark, four people in a camp can keep going. But there was no telephone (nearer than the little town to which I went for long-distance calls from the office), no social tension, no dressing up. It was really unnecessary for my wife to say that I "looked perfectly poisonous," or to point me out to a man she was introduced to in Princeton as "that hobo across the street sitting on the edge of the sidewalk by the bank."

*

We met Buck Allison on Saturday afternoon as we rode out of town, and I told my wife what a strong quick man he is, beautifully built like a Greek athlete. He was riding Nigger, a sturdy, muscled horse I'd dearly like to have. But Nigger bites; he kicked old Dan last Winter. I've seen him stamp a pig on the head, he bucks at times, and he's too high-life for me. Buck is a horseman, a gentle-spoken, soft-mannered, easygoing chap. Next day he was to ride Tom Kenyon's brown horse for me and find out what was wrong with it.

But Buck did not come next day. Had I known that Princeton would be celebrating on Saturday night I would have ridden to see. I thought the town was dead. The big copper mine shut down suddenly in November, without a day's notice, almost bankrupting the local shops. The 700 miners have been drifting away to other parts. Some remain, sullen-looking groups on the sidewalks that talk among themselves and will not move to let women pass.

There was a boxing match in Princeton on Saturday night and the loser (a stranger from Calgary) solaced himself by a private fight on the public street about ten o'clock. That, and the beer parlours and bootleggers got things started, and there were six fights and six arrests by the two local constables. Then Buck emerged from a beer parlour in all the fervour of beer and of being strong and 26, and restarted his well-known campaign for clearing Canada of aliens. He walked down the sidewalks where the Russians stand and at each group he would ask, "Are you a Bohunk or are you not?" If they answered "Yes" he hit them, and if they merely looked unpleasant and said nothing he kicked. Boy Bill at the ranch told me he saw one foreigner go clear over a car radiator after Buck hit him, and at one time Buck was driving ten of them ahead of him. The two policemen have an aversion to meeting Buck on these occasions, but it got so that they just had to take him. Handcuffs were no use, for he put one hand in front of him and one behind and they could find no way to bring his hands together. Twisting an arm was useless too, for he gently straightened the arm with the two policemen hanging on it. He was quite nice to them and they managed to trip him down so that one policeman could jam his knees on Buck's throat. A brother of Buck's, standing by, objected to that and the rest of the story is a bit mixed.

Anyway, I rode down to the Courthouse early this (Monday) morning and behind the barred window of the cooler, in the basement, I saw Buck smoking a cigaret. There was another fellow in with him, he said, and they had lots to eat. Perhaps a little reading matter? There were no police about and they wouldn't mind, anyway, so I got the reading matter and passed it in, along with some smokes and candies, and sat on the grass outside the window and talked horses with Buck, which made me late for the family pack-up, out at the shack.

But we caught this train (on which I write). Since then, when not exclaiming at the scenery, the family has been counting out-of-works free riding on the engine tender. They swarmed on when the train started, amid calls from a crowd of friends. Fourteen got off at one point, the rest may have come to Vancouver, where the idle are as thick as ever, in spite of all this travelling. If unemployment keeps up like this, through Summer, what will happen when the tens of thousands of travelling men are driven into cities by cold weather? Dole on a massive scale? Riots? When the shooting starts, I tell my wife, it might be a good idea to ship a ton of flour and a few thousand rounds of ammunition to Arcadia and stick it out there in the mountains, with horses, until the revolutions have worked themselves out. And maybe to get Buck to come along with us.

*

I was labouring one hot day, picking stones off the bridle path to town, when far down the mountain road I saw the crawling approach of a horse and rig. There was an old man in the rig, a tall, raw-boned fellow with gold spectacles and ragged clothes, leaning back contentedly against a discoloured pile of bedding and tent and pots and pans. The horse was a good horse, old too, and it sauntered along at a slow walk; the rig was very old, patched with haywire and bits of leather and string.

"Name of Brown," the man said, and I introduced myself. He was on his way to a summer's prospecting up Pitt River, had a month to travel a couple of hundred miles, and asked about lakes for fishing. Used to buy beaver skins in this country 60 years ago, he told me. Now 89 years old, he prospected for minerals ahead of C.P.R. construction in the '80s, the original staker of the copper mine at Princeton. I realized that this was the once-famous Brass Jaw Brown who sold a group of mineral claims in the boom of 1894 for a set of gold teeth (hence the name). I sat on the roadside in the hot sun, nursing my pickaxe; he lolled in his rickety rig as if it were a Rothschild barouche of 1880. We talked Klondike, the lost creek of gold he'd found up Pitt River, the unemployment situation and the young generation that couldn't get through hard times like he could with a few sacks of flour, baking powder, bacon and fishing tackle. Beneath a picture of this old man in his rig there should be written the recipe for long life of the 250-year-old Chinese sage:

> Keep a quiet heart; sit like a tortoise; walk springily like a pigeon; sleep like a dog.

I haven't seen Brass Jaw walk, but he must be some traveller, for I know they sent a search party for him up Pitt River two years ago and found him away off among the mountains, in a cave beneath a glacier living on raw flour. He babbled of a mountain of aluminum he had found. They had to carry him out because he was missing several frozen toes that he had amputated with a penknife — which is one of those bits of local colour that my wife usually prevents my telling guests at dinner. Anyhow, Brass Jaw and I became friends on sight. He might call his way of life "prospecting for minerals" and let it go at that, but I know better.

*

Talking of hard times, I met old Podunk one day. He said that when he was a little boy in Tennessee, at the time of the Civil War, raiders came to his mother's house with a wagon and cleaned it bare. His mother punched holes in a piece of metal stovepipe to make a sort of grater, and with this she shelled cobs of corn on which, with sugar she made from sugar cane, and a little salt pork, the mother and little children lived for many months. "Catch anyone doing that nowadays," he snorted. "I tell you, people haven't been living in the United States for the past six or seven years, they've been living in the Rock Candy Mountains that the hobo song speaks of, dreaming of Fairyland. Now they're in for reality. Like old man Green who came into town Friday with $45, drew his $20 old-age pension and was flat Tuesday morning. Came to me for the price of a meal just now and went straight back to the beer parlour. Said he was going home and d'you know where home is? In my shack — him." Podunk has quite a new viewpoint on drinking since the $3,000 fortune struck him. He's a fine old chap with a long white beard and knows the remote places of the mountains like a book. He and I have a trip planned some time when he isn't working for wages, which means any old time the weather's good.

* * *

June 3, 1931
Dear Mr. Denny:

I have just had the great pleasure of receiving your letter of May 21. It is nice of you to make such kind remarks about "the Graingers" and these letters from Arcadia. I enjoy writing them to you but always want to be sure (like a man who talks a lot) that I am not becoming boresome with them. Last time I wrote (crossing yours) about the family visit to the shack. My wife had not been there for nearly two years and the times of her previous visits had been ill-chosen so that mosquitoes or flies had bothered her. This time there were none and the visit was a great success, and it has pleased me a lot that of her own accord she proposes to go again in August, even to drive up herself from Vancouver. There is a beautiful park-like region round the shack and she enjoys simple country life (without mosquitoes and flies!). She took up riding again — on my buckskin Ribbons, who is now so fat that he makes an ideal cob for my wife. He looks like an enlarged children's pony, but is a gallant little mountain horse when the fat is off, and with my wife his manners are perfect. My sister-in-law (a few years ago given up several times by the doctors) was with us, active in a gentle way and almost restored to health after years of invalidism. It is this ability to "come back" after illness and accident that is so heartening a thing in life.[26]

Rheumatism you speak of, here's a recent experience of mine: For many years I have had a tendency to rheumatism around the hips, and last Winter got chilled on a night drive to Death Valley, and for over four months could only bend with rheumatic discomfort and was often with bone ache like toothache. Then I made a woollen pad lined with fluffy cotton towel and wore that round the hips night and day, which made things better but still not good. Finally I remembered how people in tropical climates wear spine pads as a protection against sunstroke, and it struck me the same idea might work against cold and draughts that stir up rheumatism, so I developed a light pad that covers my backbone as well as hips, worn over the shirt, and believe me it has taken away the rheumatism in great shape. Just a matter of steadiness of temperature for the affected region. Try this for your walking.

I was talking last evening with the wife of a missionary Bishop who had just travelled across Russia on her way to China and here. She had been astounded by the tremendous number of trainloads of cut timber she saw on her way and the multitude of working parties, each under armed guard. Mr. Pendleton came up from San Francisco on the same train as the second-in-command of the Russian Trading Company in the United States, who asked, "What harm to the U.S. lumber business did our 60,000,000 feet shipment do last year?" Mr. Pendleton said not much but it was like the old story of the camel with a cold nose. (The camel came to the tent door and asked its driver to let it in because the night was so cold. "Goodness," said the driver, "there's no room in here." "My nose is very cold," said the camel, "just let me put that in." So the camel got his nose in, and then his head, and in a little while his shoulders and so on.)

My wife and I take much interest in observing the effects of the Depression. From the pathetic side one must avert the mind; it is too sad to think of all the distress among people helplessly stranded by circumstances beyond their control. (Like the man with tears in his eyes begging our mill superintendent for a job after weeks of waiting, with wife and children to provide for.) In other aspects, hard times are doing no end of good. The brassy arrogance of easy new-made money has gone; economy and thrift are being learned again; people are getting down to realities and leaving snobberies and finding out that simple things can give as much pleasure as the high-cost-of-living things they thought essential two years ago. Will Rogers begs the President and others to quit prophesying the return of prosperity because "it brings bad luck," and gradually people are becoming convinced that they are not going to wake up some fine morning to find the Big Boom has returned. The outlook is very black. Not until people shake down to the idea that these hard times may be normal times for quite a while, and regulate themselves accordingly, would it seem possible for the return of some degree of prosperity to begin.

People here are greatly disillusioned about the leadership (they imagined during the boom) they were getting from the big U.S. industrialists, Ford and Hoover and the rest. Everywhere when people meet, you are conscious of their feeling that the ship of state is drifting rudderless. Public reputations have gone like pricked balloons. Many of these types are so objectionable to our British way of thinking that we must feel good riddance. And surely British world trade must get back some of its own when the U.S. gets into trouble such as it is in now.

* * *

June 15, 1931
Dear Mr. Denny:

In modern wars dozens of men are taken up in duties behind the lines for each man actually engaged in fighting, and it has seemed to me this year that nearly all my time and work go in strenuous preparation for trips that are so seldom made.

I saw some doggerel in a Western paper:

'Cause I'm A-Gettin' Old

When I used to start on a camping trip,
A loaf of bread and a bacon strip,
A couple of quilts, a gun or pole,
Was all that I would need.
Now, when I embark on a campin' trip
My car, loaded down from tip to tip,

Cots, rods, mattress, and quilts galore
If I had the room I'd carry more,
'Cause I'm a-gettin' old.
When I was young and in my prime,
I'd lob off some pieces of needle pine,
And lay right down and go to sleep,
Until the dawn began to creep,
Then I'd jump out with a bound,
I never had to fiddle around
Like I do now.
Now, if I lay me on a needle bed,
When I awake I'm nearly dead,
I find every needle on that tree
Has carved in initials on the side of me
'Cause I'm a-gettin' old.

This sort of thing creeps up on a person. I was horrified the other day, upon taking my stuff over to the ranch house, where they have some scales, to find my horse pack had 59 pounds of gear and food — and I thought I was travelling light! One trouble is that if my back and hips get cold I can hardly bend for rheumatism; otherwise I would like to travel really "tough". However, a little work cut five pounds off the bedding and some off the tenting and reduced the kitchen from two and a quarter pounds to twelve ounces. It is such agony for one horse to watch another eating oats that I haven't the heart to take only one nosebag. The two-and-a-half-pound nightgowns make the horses sleep soundly in rain, cold or among mosquitoes, and are worth five pounds of oats a day, at least. Otherwise further reductions in weight are in mind.

My real trouble about trips has been a shortage of horses. Two casualties last year brought me down to the big mare and the buckskin Ribbons, and while the latter is a gallant strong little horse, his occasional stumble by catching one forefoot behind the other foreleg is worse this year and I am afraid to ride him fast, especially downhill.

Thus it was that Buck Allison (freed from the cooler by fines of $28 for mixing it with the police and $5 for assaulting various Bohunks) and myself set forth to seek horses in the Dry Belt of B.C. We travelled in parts of a two-seater Ford that belonged to Buck. He knew the car so well that a hole in a tire as big as the palm of your hand meant nothing to him. Blowouts he expected and punctures came every little while. Even at dark midnight when things went wrong in the machinery Buck would crawl under the car or into the box behind and fix the trouble with a lighted match in one hand and some tool in the other. Needed tools were mostly missing, at that. Once he was nearly stumped, but I had a wire handle to a cook-pot that served as a make-shift. This was lucky for us because there are very few passers-by on these country roads this year. Commercial travellers are not travelling, and other people have not the money for gasoline.

The absence of cars, and being in a part of the country where cattle-raising is the only business, set the clock back twenty years. We met cow-punchers in fleecy chaps, Indian women riding in bright blue or scarlet blouses with coloured scarves round their hair, very picturesque. There was a roadside paddock with thirty great lowering bulls in it, throwing up dust to keep off the flies, and corrals into which a rider or two would obligingly drive a mob of horses from the range upon hearing us ask about saddle horses. But, alas, good ones are scarce nowadays, polo ponies being the only ones with any market, and most cow camps have come down to mongrel types that are half heavy workhorse. At one big cattle ranch the owner had bred some fine animals of the hunter type only to find, as he said, that "when the cowboys had broke them, they were *broke every way.*" Some were turned into fighters and buckers just so the boys could have the fun of showing off upon them; others were stove up in the legs over rocks and down steep hills in reckless riding after cattle. We had no luck, and after a three-day journey of three hundred and fifty miles, Buck and I came home.

Next weekend old Tom Kenyon's brown lulu came again into the picture and it was shown me how truly gentle he was, barring a few archings, "natural-like when a horse is just off the range-like." I had a private tip, however, that even in

Buck's capable hands there had been a scene outside the Post Office in Princeton with the brown horse bucking hard, and as this was told me my courage sank inside me. Truly beautiful horses with the fast running walk that is so much thought of are all very well, but how about being bucked off them on a cold wet morning fifty miles from anywhere, on to rocks or the stump of a tree, and saddle and pack-horse bolting for home with all the food and bedding? Not so good, at my age.

By now, indeed, it was all over the country that there was a man wanting to buy a horse and probably capable of paying for it. The price of horses rose quickly above zero. As I sit writing this on the Vancouver train, horse-owners are surely looking for me on the streets of Princeton or taking likely horses out to the ranch and asking the folks there about me or scouring the ranges to catch six of the wild ones and give them a few days' heavy riding so that they will (for the moment) be "real gentle" and suitable for an infirm, elderly sitter-on-horseback like me. Lots of them *are* real gentle if you don't put a cold saddle on them, or girth them too tight, or get on them carelessly, or let them get their heads down, or let them hear a twig of a tree crack, or see a piece of paper on the trail, or a white rock. And I've been shown a horse with little short legs in the dachshund style, a giant nearly 18 hands high like the kind lady acrobats do stunts upon in the circus, one that must have weighed three-quarters of a ton, another that quivered all over as you looked at him. All guaranteed (verbally) as gentle, fast walkers and "keep-a-going-all-day."

*

Princeton has made me a member of its Board of Trade and one evening we drove forty miles to a country convention and banquet at which Ministers of the Provincial Government were "bored and gored" (as someone said) about the condition of the country roads and the amount of unemployment relief work. It was a rattling good meeting with straight English talked and no beating about the bush. One Minister, in a fighting speech, said members of Parliament, as a class,

Letters, 1931

compared very well with their constituents, a retort that went well with the old-timers. Relief or no relief, country folk showed their feeling that they can stand world Depression better than city people. (There's deer in them there hills, and milk and eggs and beef on the ranches.) They are not like Prairie farmers who just raise wheat (in competition with Russian peasants) and need money to buy canned milk. The absence of work does not bother them, for who but crazy city people ever did want to work? Some of my friends (not many) are even putting in a little of all this spare time upon fallen fences or other ranch improvements, though this is generally considered as wasted effort. But if you want to see a worried man these days, go call upon a storekeeper in a mountain district like this where the payrolls in the mines ceased suddenly last November, with all credit accounts outstanding. No other Arcadian, of course, *ever* worries about *anything*.

*

So I reappear at the office and at once I am told privately that in forty years conditions have never even approached the desperate state they are in today in many parts of the Canadian Prairies. Drought and high winds have denuded whole regions of soil, that has blown into ridges like snow in winter. Farmers moving out of southern Saskatchewan and Alberta and going North are slaughtering stock they could not afford to move; prospects of only a half crop are general on the Prairies; militia were used to suppress some trouble at Edmonton; there was a rumour of a raid on Eaton's wholesale grocery department at Winnipeg, with some rioting. The newspapers of course suppress all the unfavourable news they can, leaving rumour to do its work. Reports of riots are particularly apt to be exaggerated. But the other information came from an excellent authority.

The porter on my train yesterday told me that the big new C.P.R. engines use only one crew out of three, so that at the little town of Revelstoke there are 250 unemployed engineers and firemen, let alone other railway men. I do not vouch for his figures. Thousands of loggers will be coming to town at the end of June with prospects of an idle summer. And there is now appearing among the unemployed a very definite trend toward Communist thinking. Hitherto, good temper has prevailed, to an astonishing degree.

* * *

September 16, 1931
Dear Mr. Denny:

I eased up on these letters for fear that they were becoming boresome, but now that some time has passed and Autumn lights the evening lamp I'll venture to inflict another on you.

*

There is a man near here who, being on part time as a machinist at the C.P.R. repair shops, has been active in cutting up logs for firewood on the beach below our windows and peddling the wood around the neighbourhood. Yesterday my sister-in-law met him, his face so set with trouble that she stopped and asked why. He had just been down to the C.P.R., he said, and read the notice posted on the gate that the repair shops were closed indefinitely. There was a crowd there and some of the married men were quite hysterical. For him it means that, with less than 20 years' service, he will never be employed there again.

*

I was astonished, in my mountain Arcadia, to find that the closing of the mines and general impoverishment had put 551 men on the relief list. Riding in and out to the high country I had never realized that there were 200 men in the "jungles" around the little town. All the prospectors and many of the ranchers I know have been working, on and off, on the Government roads, but this is only more so than usual and hadn't caught my notice much until I heard the figures. Up in that country the spirit among the men on work relief is pretty fair, as I know from my friend who is general foreman on the new transcontinental highway that is being punched through the Cascade Mountains. The Government agent who hands out the dole and passes men for the work camps told me out of his experience (good worried man!) that he found a large proportion of the junglers to be good honest working men. But here's a modern touch I got from a local minister: He was leaning over a backyard fence talking to a town resident who had been out of work for a year. The yard was bare ground. "Why don't you put in vegetables?" asked the parson. "Not worth it," said the man, "besides I'd have to have it plowed up!"

The old pioneer spirit is gone. No one intends to rough it nowadays and the young men only want to drive a car. I can remember depressions in which men would just go live upon the beach, fishing and digging clams, or exist upon their little farms, with deer meat. Nowadays they are all helpless when some payroll stops. I am so used to this that it came to me as a real heartener yesterday when a friend who runs the Association office in Vancouver where men are hired for the logging industry said emphatically, "The boys don't want any charity. They want to get work in their own line in the regular way, even if the pay is going to be less than they might earn in those Government relief works." That's the sort of thing a person wants to hear. But I'm afraid, all the same, that there's going to be trouble — in all those Coast camps to which the hundreds of drifters will be sent. Many are demoralized by 18 months of "bumming around" from one side of the continent to the other. I kind of feel that I'd be that way myself. Compared to the monotony of some labouring jobs, this carefee camping life with free railway to where you please has its pleasant side. Until the fall rains begin — without blankets or overcoats!

Well, this is enough dirge. A family man I know has just bought a piano (on instalments).

Chapter Nine
THE SPIRIT OF THE WEST

The engine puffed loud and staccato, in heavy labour. The two carriages of the little train tugged uphill yard by yard, losing way between each piston-stroke with a sudden jerk. Sleepless passengers leaned weary heads against the window-panes and stared dully at the dim scene without.

In the calm mountain air, under the blaze of stars, darknesses of stunted woods and white areas of snow made the night-covering of an open plain. Ahead, the low-lying hills gave faint sky-lines. But elsewhere, all around, the earth curved cleanly out of sight over a dim, even horizon. *Down there* the mountains we had seen at dusk had sunk. Our night-long climb had taken us to queer upper levels, to a world-roof nearer to the stars — desolate high wilderness ten thousand feet above the sea. Strange it was to see electric lights — arc-lights of mines — shining from all lonely distances across the snow, and to know that little towns and villages existed here by the fantastic choice of money-seeking men.

When bright morning came, the nightmare look of things had gone, we were among mountains again, familiar western mountains — high up ourselves upon a mountainside. The train still dragged uphill — up and up and up, insistently. Our bodies still shook to the weary jerking. But our tired minds could find relief, now that the light had come. We could smile to one another, pointing humorously at the five smoking engines of a shunted freight train. We could amuse ourselves by crowding to the carriage windows to look into valleys deep down below — valleys dotted with the signs of mining, mines working, mines abandoned, mounds (as of giant moles) beside prospectors' shafts

The Spirit of the West

and tunnels, open cuts on the hillsides. It was plain that a fierce mining boom had raged there once. Looking, we could make critical remarks to one another to air the knowledge of the art of mining that every Westerner assumes.

But mines and the interesting works of men passed out of sight again, and the train went mounting to a mere field of snow — a white valley between white mountain tops, fit themes, no doubt, for guide-book rhapsodies. In boredom we endured loop after loop of a slow zig-zag climb. Then came the end of dull endeavour. Thirteen thousand feet above the sea, and we had reached the *summit* of our pass! My heart went a-thump unpleasantly at such great altitude.

Now the painful sense of exhausted movement ceased to gnaw our patience. The chugging of the engine, the straining and creaking of the carriages, had passed away. With a fine feeling of delight, we felt the train fall into smooth continuous motion, running free upon the downward slope across a plain of snow. The plain soon hollowed to a narrow valley. We sped down that, faster and faster. The valley went deeper between hills; the hills became mountains; timber spread round us again; water ran in creek-bottoms; mine buildings showed here and there; telephone poles and electric-power lines and country roads, coming in, made the scenery tamer, and early on the bright frosty November day we came careering down to the county town of Summit County, Colorado, near which (such was my business), I was to inspect a dredge, a gold-digging dredge, and make my first expert report to "British Capital". I may as well confide the fact that I had never seen a dredge.

"What, then, is your *proper* trade or profession?" you may ask suspiciously — if you are English. Is it possible for me to explain that I, a working person, have no "proper trade or profession" without provoking you to make some wounding inferences?

Open an English Directory at "Trades and Professions" and you will find working citizens listed here, each under his business label. This man is labelled mining engineer, that man carpenter; there is a clear distinction made between the two. You know that neither man would undertake the other's work; you know that both men give prompt answers when asked their business, for in England, as in all crowded populations, workers are trained to some one form of work, to which, if they be steady men, they stick through life. Steadiness pays — it is respectable. Men who change and change from one kind of work to another damage their own reputations. Conscious of this, even the most unstable may try to give convincing answers to the plain questions, "What is your business? What do you do habitually?"

Now these ideas, this point of view, are English — English and not Western. The difference may be seen in the fact that your enquiry may have to take the form, "What are you working at *now*?" before many men out West can answer it. Working at nothing "habitually," they merely change from one "job" to another "job". As enterprising men, they look for opportunities outside, as well as in their work of the moment. Western businesses and districts, too, are subject to boom and slump. The best wages are paid now here, now there, now in this business, now in that. Therefore working-men of all kinds are encouraged to be wanderers ever at a venture — wanderers who have worked at many things.

Out West you never know what strange capacities a man may possess. Your fisherman, drying his salmon nets in the sun, may of a sudden prove an expert mechanic, and help you repair your motor-boat machinery. Your barrow-wheeling navvy may pause and tell you the right exposure for your photograph of the railway cut. "Worked two years in a photographer's," he explains. The same man in his time may have been mining in Alaska, logging on the B.C. coast, tending a saloon bar in the city of Seattle, driving team in Idaho, working in machine-shops in Tucson near to Mexico — and be on the point, now, of "going in for ranching." Bees or tomatoes are sure money-makers, may be his argument. You wonder what he knows of either.

You gasp, if you are from Europe, to see a man willing to risk his little all upon so frail a scheme. But stay and watch him go to work, and, hit or miss, you will see the man's stock-in-trade — self-reliance, weird power of effective make-shift, fearless tackling of unknown difficulties. He will show, to some extent, "the spirit of the West". There are a great number of

The Spirit of the West

such men about. They fill the camps. Camp life, therefore, on its social side, is much the same in a Western place. Men are men-of-the-world — this Western world — and working beside them, living with them, listening to them, a man will add to his own experience a sort of vague knowledge of the whole West — knowledge of its far places and many businesses.

In my own case (for to that I have been leading you by these remarks) such education had been going on for years. I had lived in camps, worked at this and at that, gained, at second-hand, many a shallow experience of work and things and places I had never seen. So it happened that I felt myself prepared to understand gold-dredging and its problems. Had I not known men who had worked on dredges down in California? Had I not worked myself — tunnelling in gold-bearing gravel, and worked hydraulicking? Was not dredging, after all, merely another process for separating gold from gravel? And as I, a Western Canadian from Victoria, who never before had visited the Western States, alighted at my destination that fine November day, and walked up the main street of the county town of Summit County, I felt myself in known surroundings, among known men (groups of lounging miners eyeing a stranger curiously), bound upon familiar business.

And so the best hotel, in that town of one thousand souls, proved equally familiar. I found its damaged wall-papers blazing in the usual way with green and gold and dull maroon, cherubs and roses festooned on the low ceilings. The fine glass and polished wood-work of a bar-room made contrast with the usual group of noisy men in muddy boots and overalls, torn coats and broad slouch hats. A hotel-office-and-public-room contained the usual loafers sitting in deep silence round a red-hot stove in a stuffy atmosphere at fever-heat.

And the talk of an old-timer, whose silence I contrived to break during the afternoon, seemed like an echo of talk heard before, in old mining districts up North in Cassiar. It dealt with mines and mining, I need hardly say. Words on any other subject rarely cross an old-timer's lips.

"Yes," he said, "this here has been a great camp in its time. Thirty-six million dollars have been took out of the shallow diggins in the gulches round this town. Why, there's gold everywhere! Gold in the bed-rock, gold on the hillsides, gold in every yard of the valley bottoms. Look at the values these here dredges are getting in the deep ground that the old placer miners couldn't handle — fifty cents a yard in the channel and an average of twenty-five over the whole body of gravel. How does values like them strike you? There was good colours even in the ground dug from the cellar underneath this room we're sitting in. You go 'long to Sam Hunt who keeps a jewelry store down the street and ask him to show you them specimens he's got."

It is, I think, a foolish thing to look at nuggets. It warps one's judgment of a mining place. My judgment of the prospects of a dredge in Summit County, Colorado, was warped that afternoon by the beauty of Sam Hunt's specimens. They took my breath away — crystalline gold, gold in long wires like metal trimmings from a lathe, fine wire gold in tangled masses like a golden moss. They came, in these, their natural states, from rock nearby the town. I doubt if such are found elsewhere in all the world. And then the pile of heavy metal slugs — gold nuggets, water-worn, washed from creek bottoms in the neighbourhood — that Sam Hunt poured upon the counter of his store.

"Aren't you scared of being held up and robbed?" I asked. As an inhabitant of peaceful Canada I had no clear idea of the amount of lawlessness to be expected in a Colorado town. "No," said the jeweller, "this country is quiet enough nowadays. Right in the town here there hasn't been a hold-up for seven or eight years — not since them two fellows held up the hotel." On that occasion, it appears, the hotel proprietor and some dozen friends were sitting in the gambling-room at cards. Two masked men, armed with shot-guns, rushed in suddenly through different doors. The players threw up their hands, and "froze" motionless; the robbers cleared their pockets and the tables. One gun went off (so nervous was its holder) and blew a hole in the bar-room ceiling; both men rushed out into the black night. Next day the marshal and another man ran the two robbers to bay — in an old cabin in the hills. There was some shooting — and then the grim sight (to searching citizens) of four dead men upon a cabin floor.

The Spirit of the West

This type of bold hold-up, however, belonged to the heroic age of Summit County. Today, robbery at the revolver's mouth is an affair for lonely neighbourhoods. The *demi-monde*, for example, in the outskirts of the county town, have been held up three times within the past twelve months by robbers never found. And that reminds me that I have not yet impressed you with the great decorum reigning in the town. To within a few weeks of my visit, everything had been "wide open." Faro and poker, and other forms of sport, had been running "right along, day and night, *never stop*" — to the great benefit of the hotels and other establishments. But one day the local parson (a parson in that town — O problem of the fly in amber!) had worked himself up and, standing in the district attorney's office, had demanded the enforcement of the law. The district attorney had been obliged, poor man, to "go 'round and put a stop to all the fun for a while." The hotels submitted gracefully by way of humouring the law — for a while. There was a lull. Then an impatient someone with the fine directness of retort that meets one in the Western states, dynamited the parson's church — "a piece of blamed foolishness." The indignation of decent citizens caused a wave of purity to sweep the place; gambling was stopped forever, and the *demi-monde* expelled — a short distance further from the town.

Now all this had happened several weeks before my visit. For weeks the deadly dullness of the evening had cast its gloom upon men's lives. A man cannot be always "getting drunk" — there are limits to the pleasure. There is a point, too, at which cigars lose interest, and Denver newspapers, and the cud of mining talk that has been often talked before. Even a judge fresh from a victory at the polls may weary of three volumes of *The World's Great Orators* in spite of what book-agents say. So men of this county town, facing the boredom of their leisure time, asked one another the stale question, "How the blank is a man to amuse himself after his day's work is done?" and in the blue absence of an answer they asked themselves something else: "How shall it profit a man — such self-inflicted virtue?"

I found that there had arisen a general feeling that "the thing had gone far enough," moderation in reform being as good as moderation in other things. The town, in fact, had prepared itself to start again upon a course of moderation in social sports, and already a small, quiet card game had begun to solace the evening hours at my hotel.

I have touched on the subject of the "hold-up" for the sake of local colour, robber-with-a-gun being a staple news-item in the Western press. In the same sort of country, in the same sort of life — in Western Canada, this form of law-breaking has no vogue at all. It was stamped out at its beginning by a hanging judge in early mining days. "Bad men" coming into Canada shun the least thought of "gun-play." Is it not of interest that the mere crossing of an imaginary line, the mere contact with different sentiment, should effect such moral reformation?

In the Western states, the "bad man" does not arouse a permanent shocked hostility. After his crime he is hunted with momentary fury. Then public opinion calms down, and people resign themselves to look upon him and his kind as inevitable nuisances. The "hold-up," in particular, has much the same standing in the West that burglary has in London. It is a prosaic thing that happens. Sometimes, indeed, it is the work of intelligent men with a sense of humour. I think there is rather a pleasant touch about a recent hold-up of a mine manager. Absurdly foolish, he had talked about a gold brick that he was about to take from his mine to the town where there was a bank. *Of course*, when he came to make the journey he was held up — he and his wife in their buggy, his advance and rear guards (men armed with Winchesters) on their horses. You may imagine these people's hands shooting (with action quite automatic) to arm's length above their heads at the sudden unexpected menace of careless rifles pointing at their stomachs. But there was nothing *tragic* about the hold-up men. "Don't get scared, Mary," they called reassuringly to the manager's wife, "we ain't a-going to hurt anybody. Now then, friend John, dig up that gold brick please." So rueful John handed over the brick and (as the story goes) "the laugh was against him"; and that was the end of an incident that might have curdled a melodrama by its "strength".

The Spirit of the West

So much for the hold-up, subject of many amusing stories, a subject that, by demand of convention and gloating publishers, gains such airs of blood and thunder when in print. Peaceable you and I would lead the same uneventful lives in Colorado that we lead at present in our suburb of an English town. We would hear of hold-ups, aye, and occasional deaths by shooting; we would meet the men who had figured in such affrays — with the same tepid interest that we now have for motor-car accidents. Like me, you might find it dull to take polite drinks with a hospitable doctor, who in the same bar-room, not many years before, had shot and killed an unarmed man, a married man with a very reasonable grievance. The doctor may have been nearly lynched; his escape through the law may have cost him two thousand dollars.

"Well, and what then?" you would ask, were you a citizen of Summit County. Like me again you might be introduced, in a commonplace hotel office, to an ordinary-looking stranger, a clean-shaven, gentle-mannered man with the mild attitudes and beseeching smiles that curates with spectacles so often have. You might be so introduced — and feel like me but slight curiosity. Yet surely (one would have supposed) there should be something queer in thus meeting — in a white people's country in this modern time — a personage who had gone to Telluride as mine-manager, to succeed a murdered man (murdered with two of his foremen), who had set himself up in opposition to the labour organization that had caused the murder; who had had the side of his house blown in and been himself blown out of bed by dynamite used with intent to kill; who had seen it proved that for the murder of such men as himself, juries were afraid (or unwilling) to convict; who had helped, nevertheless, to break the hostile power; who had (at the time of meeting) but recently emerged from the daily peril of his life.

The trouble is that the trivial contact you and I (as residents of Summit County) would have with such strange matters and such unusual men would give us no concern or thrill. We should go about our business — which might perhaps be gold-digging with a dredge — and think uninterruptedly about mining and our own peaceable affairs.

Chapter Ten
RIDING DOWN FROM CHILCOTIN

Some thirty-six years ago, my wife and her sister visited the Churches in Alberta. It appears that the young ladies fell off wild steers and were run away with by racehorses in a way that Mr. Church still remembers as unusual in those Victorian days. Later, as farmers came in and the open range was fenced, the Churches moved on to freer country in northern B.C.[27]

Twelve years ago one of their daughters married Moore, a tall Bostonian who had been in the Canadian service in the War. The couple set off with saddle and pack-horses until near Tatlayoko Lake (just behind the high Coast Mountains) they found land that could be farmed. Today half a dozen families, thirty-five souls in all, live in the little valley, each with a few acres of cleared land amid the surrounding jackpine forest, a log cabin built low with a foot of gravel on the roof (for warmth in winter), some straggling barns and corrals. These farms produced very little; the people lived chiefly on deer meat. Deer were everywhere. The procedure, for form's sake, is to get from some distant game warden an out-of-season permit to kill one deer. This will be the deer hung in your larder when the game warden makes one of his rare inspection trips. You have a little canning rig and can deer meat, which is very good this way. There is also cows' milk and eggs, with flour and oatmeal bought at the stores at Williams Lake, when there happens to be money available from the sale of the few head of horses and cattle that they raise.

*

Riding Down from Chilcotin

One evening in April, I took a Canadian Pacific train, got off next morning at Ashcroft in the Dry Belt and in a few hours, by auto stage, reached Williams Lake, 150 miles north on the Cariboo Road. This village is the railhead of a Government railway, known chiefly for the desperate race that is the feature of its annual Rodeo — a race in which cowboys dash at full speed down the steep rock face of a mountain. There are always casualties. One year five horses were killed and three men went to hospital.

At Williams Lake I was met by Mrs. Moore. She had driven in 160 miles with two cowboys who had spent the Winter shooting wild horses for the bounty, and she drove me (and a load of groceries) back to her house in two days over some of the worst mudholes I have ever imagined a car could pull through. After crossing the Fraser River (most picturesque), we rose up to the high, park-like Chilcotin plateau and lunched at Mr. Moon's. He and Bert Thomas came out together in 1891, and I was the carrier of messages between them. A jolly, red-faced, typical country Englishman was Mr. Moon — a very likable chap, like John Bull. He would do fine at a Christmas dinner, old style, has done well here and is very well-to-do.

We then drove to a side road where Mrs. Moore was to pick a horse in payment of an old debt (a cow given years ago to an impoverished rancher). She got a little rat of a horse, the mean man explaining that he had *sold* all his good ones!

From there it was 80 miles to Alexis Creek, where we spent a pleasant evening with friends of Mrs. Moore who have a big ranch and are prosperous, hard workers. There is a tiny settlement at Alexis Creek, with a doctor and so on. Next morning off we drove again, stopping at one ranch for coffee and cake and then taking an appalling side road — just cart tracks showing here and there through woods. By supper we reached the Moores' place, in the little valley that ends at Tatlayoko Lake, beyond which rose the great white mountains of the Coast Range, twelve and thirteen thousand feet high, a fine sight.

Summer and Winter, the children ride horseback to a log building that is the schoolhouse where a girl from Vancouver struggles to control the older boys. Families take turns to ride, 25 miles each way, for the weekly mail that reaches Tatla Lake.

Mrs. Moore, a lithe, jolly little woman, granddaughter of a celebrated Oxford professor, mother of two children, herds the family cattle while her husband plows the fields. Each year when rodeos are held the lady borrows a racehorse or two from the Indians, rides (say) a hundred miles to the meeting place, camping as she goes, races bareback with her knees tucked into a surcingle, splits the prize money she wins with the racehorse owners, and returns home to preside at meals as a well-educated ladylike person should.

Mrs. Moore made a two-day journey last Fall over the hills to an Indian Reserve and bought me a grey mare from an Indian, Eagle Lake Henry, a very superior Indian whose stock was half Arab. The mare was ten years old, but very lively for her age, well-preserved and docile as a kitten. She had won a number of saddle-horse races in the northern country.

I stayed a day with the Moores. The husband is a big chap, very likeable, rather inert as a rancher. He does the farming, Mrs. Moore runs the cattle. Everyone in the country calls her Dolly. She is a champion runner and might have trained for the Olympic Games, and she is a rider of racehorses "from away back." I liked her immensely — she is the real country girl, the genuine horse athlete, competent as Paderewski on his piano.

I was in a hurry to get back to country where occasional telegraph lines keep one in touch with business troubles. As I had over 400 miles to go to Princeton where my horses live, and the mountain trails were likely to confuse a stranger, this athletic lady and a neighbouring 17-year-old French-Canadian girl rounded up their horses to guide me for two days by short-cuts through the hills. I borrowed a pack-horse from the Moores, put a fine baked chunk of deer meat, brown bread and oatmeal in the pack, and we started off.

The dim trails we followed rose to a plateau country with lots of swamps in it. We travelled over rather dreary jackpine country at 4,000-feet elevation, snow still there in patches, the trail boggy with the melting of it. We skirted mountain meadows and lakes on whose swamp grass cattle live, and came out upon more open range where wild-horse killers had been at work. Over a thousand head had been shot for the Government bounty. They were a nuisance, eating up the range, mostly inbred animals of no value. Mrs. Moore was rather sad about it — she used to like to ride up there and watch the wild horses play.

Eagle Lake Henry was away from home, so we camped the first night at his place in the hills, using the empty corrals to graze the horses. It was very pleasing to see the mare when we came to the grazing grounds around Eagle Lake, where she was raised. At each new place we came to she danced prettily with her fine taut limbs. At one favourite spot where horses were used to gathering she made little hops in the air, all four feet off the ground. She curvetted as horses did in the pictures of Louis 14th and nobles of his times. A charming mare, so keen, so vigorous and yet so gentle. No kicking or rough stuff.

Next day we went through dull jackpine, then through open park country with lakes and wide grasslands. We passed a bog in which a poor cow lay mired; it must have been there at least a week with its starving little calf standing on the bank above the mire. It was a dirty job, my part of it lugging on the cow's tail, and I said "ugh" involuntarily, but Mrs. Moore was most efficient.

That evening we reached the Purdues' place — two brothers of this name live a few miles apart. At this one's place there was, sitting with bowed head by the stove, overwhelmed with shyness, an Indian girl, of whom no-one took the slightest notice. She sidled up to a remote corner of the table, where we ate, and helped wash up. She generally effaced herself, but was evidently a member of the establishment. French-Canadians the brothers are — one in a magnificent rakish hat. Both are wonderful at breaking horses. A man named Fraser had dropped in to get two broken, and they halter broke them while he waited. Our party made several camps under the trees that were around the cabins. I had a lost horseshoe replaced and Mrs. Moore borrowed a racehorse from the Purdues for a meet on July 1. Next day Mrs. Moore and the girl and Mr. Fraser with his horses went homeward. We had come 56 miles in two days to the Purdues and I was surprised to find this "short cut" across the hills meant 60 more miles for me to go.

Next morning I set off alone along what the brothers called (for lack of another word) a wagon road — a sort of goat track through the woods — leading me to the big Chilco Ranch 60 miles away.

I got off next morning at 7, and was in trouble with the tired pack-horse. I tried driving him ahead, and the lead rope got jammed under the pack, and I thought we were in for a wreck, but by good luck I got him to cool off and was able to repack. Then an Indian family came by, the lady with a brilliant scarf round her head (green) and bright orange blouse, rather effective. She had a few words of English, but her man had none. The baby was on the pommel of papa's saddle, while five pack-horses were driven loose.

At 12 I made the Stobie place — a fenced pasture in the hills, and let the hungry horses graze while I thought about nothing while toasting my toes in the bright sun as I sat doing horseguard out in the hot pasture.

After coffee I went on. At 5:15 the horses were a bit tired so at 7 we stopped at a swamp where there looked to be a good little lake. But when I went down to get water there was a bog all around the lake and I couldn't get to the water. I shared the last three pounds of oats between the two horses, myself too thirsty to eat. A very "dry camp." To bed at 9, meaning to make an early start at 2:30, but slept till 4:30. Off at 5:30, with no breakfast or drink for anyone. Horses fresh again, and I had found out at last that the pack-horse's dragging on the rope was probably due to a crick in the neck caused by my strenuous leading of him from the halter. When this was changed to leading from the neck, he was vastly relieved, and came willingly.

This horse business is like the rest of life — full of mishap and accident, toil, dust, hunger and thirst, sprained fingers and fatigue. You plug grimly along say for two solid hours after your muscles have had more than enough in order to reach horsefeed; then water turns out to be unreachable because of bog around it; so you have a dry supperless camp and next

Riding Down from Chilcotin

morning must ride three hours before reaching water and getting breakfast, and so on. Making do with three or four hours sleep, you will struggle for hours in the saddle next day, not to lose consciousness and fall. Or the night may turn extra cold and keep you semi-shivering and half awake until you rise, stiff in the joints, at 2:30, and then when the sun comes up and warms you there is the aforesaid struggle to keep awake and not fall off.

Toil of this kind suits me well. Without it I should be crippled with rheumatism, indigestion and melancholia. With it I eat moderately, walk sprightly like a pigeon (as the old Chinese philosopher recommended) and am immune to all depression, getting zest out of existence.

*

After miles of trotting, we came down out of the hills to where two Indian women and some kids and all kinds of dogs were having breakfast at the mouth of a battered tent. I had to repack there, as the pack-horse was so thin that the pack slipped back over where his stomach ought to have been. Just then an Indian man came in driving seven pack- and saddle horses, and he had a word or two of English, whereas the women had just looked without speaking when I saluted them, and asked how far to Chilco Ranch. He thought five miles. I rode for an hour and 45 minutes at a good trot before I made it (say 11 miles), but one can never take Indian mileage seriously anyway. There was quite a collection of buildings at Chilco Ranch — the owner, Spencer (an Australian), had gone off his head and shot someone and killed himself last Fall. Mrs. Spencer was away, the ranch storekeeper told me. Then he remembered meeting me once at a meeting in 1918 when I was up this way on Government business. So the hungry horses went into a nice cool barn out of the heat of the morning (bright blue sky and hot sun) and had all the oats and hay they could stuff (I must go and water them now). I filled up in the kitchen with six cups of warm milk and coffee and a plateful of hotcakes.

Mr. Orford (an intelligent man) and I discussed the world's affairs and the Depression, and here I am writing in the store while he sells things to one or two cowboys and Indians. Business is bad, but these folks hardly know what real depression is. I exchanged wires with Miss Browning over the phone to Williams Lake (i.e., phone to there from this ranch and then telegraph to Vancouver). The reply came within two hours, everything OK at the office and nothing to go back for yet. This evening I'll ride out on the road to Big Creek and camp by the roadside, so as to breakfast with the Church family tomorrow morning.

In the country through which I rode it was as if Time had been put back 30 years. Men and women rode saddle horse, not in cars; there were Indians who spoke little or no English; moneyless families clearing new ground and living on simple food; old-time hospitality to the stranger. At Big Creek I stopped for a dance to which people came from 80 miles around on horseback, by rig, motor trucks or cars. It was a picturesque affair, kerosene cans of coffee boiling over campfires, a midnight supper, fiddle music played with real kick, and dancing until 7 a.m. just as in the old days. Some of the cowboys brought Australian wine (of all things!), but there were no casualties that the ladies could object to. I took the news of the party with me as I rode south. It helped conversation at meals, at ranches and cow-camps, etc., to which I put in for horsefeed.

When I met Indians or cowboys the grey mare was an immediate introduction. They all seemed to know her. Some knew the pack-horse — "Eagle Lake Henry's mare," someone would say with a quick glance at the brand on her flank and another glance at Indian Juke's brand on the pack-horse. Then they would give me a sort of thoughtful scrutiny to make sure that I was not a horse thief beating my way out of that country by back trails. I looked dirty enough for anything and unshaven, my clothes a bit ragged and horse gear old and worn. One old rancher gruffly let me use his barn but never asked me in to the house when the dinner gong was struck. At most places, however, they made me welcome, and this saved the horses and me the labour of packing oats on the journey. But why I should prefer to flop my blankets at night out under the stars on the nearest clean spot to the stable door, instead of sleeping in a bed in a room with shut windows, was a thing these ranchers could never make out.

Intelligent men, many of these back-country ranchers were, and surprisingly aware, by radio and by weekly mail, of what the rest of the world was doing. They have been spending less money since the Depression started because the price of cattle is lower than it was — but spending money was never much of a feature in their lives. Apart from that they know by hearsay or by reading that times are bad but deer meat is as plentiful as usual, and cows and chickens continue to produce as they have always done, so what is this Depression anyway?

At Clinton I'll leave the grey mare for a time and go to Vancouver to check up on business matters, returning to make the distance from Clinton to Princeton some other weekend. This is the life! Lovely weather, no flies, nice horse, old-style country life, pioneer conditions. It renews my forgotten youth.

FOOTNOTES

1. Henry William Allerdale Grainger (1848-1923). Born in Cumberland, England, he was a journalist, stockbroker and politician who spent most of his life in Australia, and also served as Agent-General for the colony in London between 1901 and 1905. He was married to Isabella King Martin of Devon, and Martin was their only child.
2. Dorothy Browning, Grainger's secretary during his business career.
3. Vermilion Forks was the early name for Princeton.
4. The CPR's Kettle Valley line, which ran from Vancouver to the West Kootenays by way of Hope, the Coquihalla Pass, Princeton and Penticton.
5. Grainger had known Herbert Heald "Bert" Thomas since he was appointed a provincial Forest Ranger in 1912. Born in Gloucestershire, England, in 1874, Thomas had arrived in B.C. in 1892. He worked as a surveyor's assistant on the Dewdney Trail over the Coast Range to the Interior, and at the Copper Mountain mine. In 1902 he married Grace Allison, daughter of Susan and John Fall Allison, pioneer ranchers in the Similkameen. In 1912 he bought the 600-acre property at One-Mile Creek, five miles northeast of Princeton, which Grainger refers to. It had once belonged to John Fall Allison's brother William. Bert Thomas was a well-read man who became one of Grainger's closest friends. Grace Thomas died at the ranch in 1969 and her husband, who had at one time worked as a foreman on the Hope-Princeton Highway, lived another four years, dying at the age of 99. He had lived in Princeton for 76 years. The couple had four sons and Bert also had three

brothers living in the area. The Thomas and Allison families formed a large clan, with which Grainger was closely involved from 1928 to his death in 1941. When Susan Allison died in 1937 at the age of 92 she left 11 children, 65 grandchildren and 17 great grandchildren, a number of whom lived in the Princeton area. Her daughters Grace and Carrie were married to Bert Thomas and his brother William. Two other daughters, Susan Louisa and Angela Amelia, were married to Princeton men, Albert Johnston and Henry McDiarmid. Sons Alfred E. and Harold H. Allison also lived in the area. (Information on Bert Thomas and the Allisons was obtained from the Okanagan Historical Society Report, No. 38, 1974, and *A Pioneer Gentlewoman in British Columbia: The Recollections of Susan Allison*, edited by Margaret A. Ormsby.)

6. Macauley was a professor from Cambridge who visited Grainger.

7. Grainger's niece, Evelyn Grey, who had recently been stricken by tuberculosis.

8. While working for the Forest Branch, Grainger suffered a severe case of fallen arches after hiking through swamps and mountain snow in the Kitimat area wearing inadequate shoes. After his recovery he began wearing moccasins whenever he could.

9. Lumberman Harvey Reginald MacMillan had suffered a near-fatal bout of tuberculosis at age 23 and spent almost two years recovering; Leonard P. Andrews, a former member of the Forest Branch, from 1926 to 1929 was manager of the Vancouver Island logging operations of Bloedel, Stewart and Welch.

10. Dart was the family nickname for Grainger's wife, Mabel.

11. The Pendletons were a B.C. logging family. Ross was manager of Alberni-Pacific. Jack MacMillan was no kin to H.R.

12. W.J. VanDusen was a Forest Service officer before becoming one of MacMillan's business partners.

13. Address of Grainger's company office in Vancouver.

14. Lafon was a Forest Service employee and later business associate of Grainger; "your father" was Ralph Grey, married

to Mabel Grainger's sister, Winifred, and hired by Grainger in various capacities over the years; Dr. G.F. Strong was Grainger's doctor and a leading Vancouver medical figure.

15. Jura and Belfort were two small train stations on the hill above Princeton where the Kettle Valley line track wound in loops to maintain grade.

16. Constance Grey was Grainger's niece, Eve's older sister.

17. Jean was H.R. MacMillan's daughter.

18. Williams won the 100- and 200-metre sprints at the 1928 Olympics in Amsterdam.

19. Austin C. Taylor, prominent Vancouver businessman and sportsman.

20. The doctor's death sentence for Old Dan proved to be premature; he had a few good years left.

21. The newspaperman was Cecil Scott of the *Vancouver Province*, not Bruce Hutchison as has been written elsewhere. Hutchison went to the area a few years later with another party.

22. Willard Albert Davis, known to all as "Podunk," came from Kentucky and had driven cattle in Wyoming on his way to B.C. He first negotiated the Hope-Princeton trail around 1890. Twinkle-eyed, ruddy-cheeked, with a flowing white beard, Davis was one of Princeton's best-known citizens and most knowledgeable about the surrounding mountain country. Naturalist Hamilton Mack Laing, who spent his honeymoon in a log cabin owned by Davis on 12-Mile Creek in 1927, said he was "about 70 but he climbs the hills and hauls the horse up after him like a youth of 40-odd. A good old scout even though he thinks bears are hatched from eggs and that deer never lie down while the moon is above the horizon, and fries certain unmentionable parts of the buck that I give to the Whiskey Jacks." (Quoted by Richard Mackie in *Hamilton Mack Laing: Hunter-Naturalist*.)

23. The Flavelle brothers' cedar mill at Port Moody.

24. "Miss Allen" was actually Mary Warburton, widely known to the public as "Nurse Warburton" through newspaper reports of her disappearance and rescue in the fall of 1926 after five weeks in the mountains. Scottish-born, Miss

Footnotes

Warburton had emigrated to B.C. in 1923 and worked as a nurse in Vancouver. She had started hiking from Hope and was bound for Penticton to pick fruit. It is not clear why Grainger did not use her real name, but there is little doubt that he actually encountered her in the same area a couple of years later. Miss Warburton was found by a policeman and the legendary Podunk Davis (see note 22 above) when hope had been given up after a late September snowfall and they were searching for her body. Down to 80 pounds, the nurse, in her mid-fifties, had chewed leaves and fungus to stay alive, sleeping by day with her feet in a knapsack and staying awake all night. She spent a week in hospital in Princeton but was back in the area the following year, telling a reporter: "There is something irresistible about the Hope Mountains. One feels when one gazes over that sea of country, from a lofty summit, something grand — angelic, as it were ... it's wonderful. Such freedom, after being penned up in the sickroom, nursing. This is the most glorious country I know." The reporter described her as "a little woman, sparely built, fair-complexioned," with rosy cheeks and sparkling eyes who looked younger than her 57 years. In 1930 she disappeared while hiking from Squamish to North Vancouver and no trace was ever found. (From Vancouver *Province*, Sept. 2, 1928, p. 7; and Cecil Clark, *Colonist* Islander Magazine, Oct. 19, 1972, p. 3.)

25. Norman Spalding was a cousin of Arthur Spalding of Pender Island. Arthur was the uncle of Mabel Grainger and of Grainger's friend Leonard Higgs.

26. Winifred Grey, sister of Mabel Grainger and mother of Evelyn and Constance.

27. Grainger wrote two versions of "Riding Down from Chilcotin" and this is an amalgam. Herbert and Richard Church emigrated from England in 1886 and began ranching south of Calgary. The two young brothers were among the first to homestead in that area and became expert cattlemen and horsebreeders at their "Hadley Ranch." (The Church family is profiled by Patrick Dunae in *Gentlemen Emigrants*.)

INDEX

Allen, Miss, 68-71, 73, 116, 117
Allison, Buck, 80, 85, 86, 92, 93
Allison George, 9-11, 16-22
Bonafia, Charlie, 42
Boyd, Jack, 35
Brown, Brass Jaw, 87, 88
Browning, Dorothy, ix, x, 3, 4, 13, 17, 112, 114
Church family, 106, 112, 117
Davis, Podunk, 64, 65, 75, 88, 116, 117
Denny, C. R., viii
Grainger, H. W. A., ix, 114
Grainger, Mabel, 14, 21, 32, 33, 83, 89
Grey, Constance, 21, 83, 116
Grey, Evelyn, ix, 115
Grey, Winifred, 83, 89, 117
Haynes, Bill, 2
Hemingson, W., 4
Henry, Eagle Lake, 108
Hill, Newsy, 56, 57
Jimmy, Eagle Lake, 1
Kenyon, Tom, 80-82
Lafon, John, 13, 115

MacMillan, H. R., vi, vii, 12, 13, 115
MacMillan, Jack, 12, 115
MacMillan, Jean, 18, 22, 116
Manning, E. C., viii
Martin, Roy, 38
McDiarmid family, 59, 60, 115
McDiarmid, Henry, 42, 60, 115
McGregor, Dan, 48, 52, 53, 62, 65, 76, 81, 84
Moon, Mr. 107
Moore, 106
Moore, Dolly, 106-109
Norton, Ranger, 4, 5
Orford, Mr. 112
Owen, Bill, 26
Pendleton, Sr., 12, 115
Pigott, 16, 26
Spalding, Norman, x, 117
Thomas, Bert, vii, viii, 6, 8-11, 15, 16, 18, 20-22, 38, 41, 45, 46, 48, 114, 115
Thomas, Grace, 9, 21, 46, 114
VanDusen, 13, 115
Watcom, Tom, 2
Williams, Percy, 34, 116
Wilson, Buck, 26